LANGUAGE WORKS 10

English Literacy Resource

Robert Cutting
Robin Pearson

LanguageWorks 10 Workbook

Cutting, Robert, 1952–
  LanguageWorks 10 workbook

(Prentice Hall language)
Supplement to: ResourceLines 9/10/Robert Dawe, Barry Duncan, Wendy Mathieu.
ISBN 0-13-026293-5

1. English language – Problems, exercises, etc. – Juvenile literature.
2. English language – Grammar – Problems, exercises, etc. – Juvenile literature.
I. Dawe, Robert T. (Robert Thomas), 1948– . ResourceLines 9/10. II. Title. III. Series.

PE1112.D297 1999 Suppl. 2   428   C00-931761-9

Prentice-Hall, Inc., Upper Saddle River, New Jersey
Prentice-Hall International, Inc., London
Prentice-Hall of Australia, Pty., Ltd., Sydney
Prentice-Hall of India Pvt., New Delhi
Prentice-Hall of Japan, Inc., Tokyo
Prentice-Hall of Southeast Asia (PTE) Ltd., Singapore
Editora Prentice-Hall do Brasil Ltda., Rio de Janeiro
Prentice-Hall Hispanoamericana, S.A., Mexico

ISBN 0-13-026293-5

Director of Secondary Publishing: Paula Goepfert
Publisher: Mark Cobham
Project Manager: Sara Jane Kennerley
Editorial Consultant: Robin Pearson
Production Editor: Kendra McKnight
Research Editor: Linda Sheppard
Production Co-ordinator: Sandra Magill
Cover/Interior Design: Alex Li
Cover photographs: Digital imagery® copyright 1999 PhotoDisc, Inc.

Printed and bound in Canada
8 9 WC 09 08

LANGUAGE*WORKS* 10

TABLE OF CONTENTS

Unit 5 Putting It Together!   **111**

Unit 6 Review and Reference 137

WELCOME TO LANGUAGEWORKS

Welcome to *LanguageWorks 10*! This workbook will increase your understanding of the English language and will help develop your writing skills. It is made up of the following six units:

- Preparing for Tests in Reading and Writing
- Vocabulary
- Spelling, Capitalization, Punctuation
- Grammar and Usage
- Putting It Together!
- Review and Reference

Units 2 to 5 begin with a **Focus On** page. This is similar to a *pretest* on the contents of the lessons that follow. At the end of each unit, there are **Check Up** pages that evaluate how much you have learned. Extra help is given in the **Review** pages in Unit 6. Unit 1 will help you prepare for the Reading and Writing Tests in Grade 10.

Whether you follow each lesson, one page to the next, or concentrate on the lessons that will help you the most, *LanguageWorks 10* will be a valuable resource during your second year in secondary school!

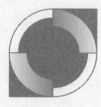

Unit 1

Preparing for Tests in Reading and Writing

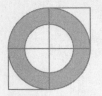

Introduction

Welcome to "Preparing for Tests in Reading and Writing." This section of *LanguageWorks 10* will help you to practise the specific skills on which you could be assessed in a test of reading and writing. You will have opportunities to determine your own strengths and weaknesses, and to learn from your mistakes. As well as practising test-taking strategies, students should also be encouraged to read, as an excellent way to prepare for reading and writing tests.

This section is set up in the following way:

Reading

- Reading Skills to Be Tested
  - Comprehension
  - Inference
  - Interpretation
  - Explanation

Writing

- Writing Skills to Be Tested
  - Writing a summary
  - Writing to express an opinion
  - Writing a news report
  - Writing an information paragraph

Sample Reading and Writing Tasks

This is a series of eight selections, followed by questions, for extra practice in test-taking. The articles relate to a variety of subject areas, including history, mathematics, media, civics, science, health, careers, and literary topics. The readings are one page each, with charts, graphics, and informational writing.

Reading

When students read, they rely upon skills that they developed at a very young age. There are several methods of teaching reading, and each has its advantages, but no one method works best for each student. The advantage that students in secondary school have, is that they can examine the methods they are using. They can also modify them to read more effectively and to understand more of what they are reading. Sometimes this is a matter of speed, concentration, or just plain practice. The very best preparation for any kind of reading test is for the student to practise reading.

Reading Skills to Be Tested

• **Comprehension:** reading to understand information

• **Inference:** reading to draw conclusions based on facts

• **Interpretation:** reading to decide the meaning of something

• **Explanation:** reading to account for or give reasons for something

---

Tips!

• It is an excellent idea to <u>underline</u> key words in the piece that you are reading. Don't hesitate to make notes on the reading passage—these will help you to better answer the questions.

• In the reading section of the test, you are not being tested for your writing, but rather for your correct answers. Therefore, unless you are asked to write in paragraph form, you may simply list the information required for short answers.

Read the article "Judging Prime Ministers," and answer the questions that follow over the next four pages. Notice that the questions are divided according to the types of reading skills which they address: **comprehension**, **inference**, **interpretation**, and **explanation**.

Judging Prime Ministers

Mackenzie King was Canada's longest-serving prime minister. In his time, he was not loved, but he was respected. In the decades after his death, however, he became the most ridiculed of Canadian politicians. At best, he was seen as dull, dithering, and timid. At worst, he was described as a "waffler," a "political weasler," and a "superstitious lunatic." What caused King's fall from favour? The cause lay largely in the revelations about his private life.

In 1997, *Maclean's* asked 25 prominent historians to rank Canada's prime ministers. To the surprise of many readers, Mackenzie King was voted the best. A year later, another *Maclean's* poll chose King as the number-one nation-builder in Canada's history. He was praised for his intelligence and for his ability to keep the nation together. What had caused the rehabilitation of King? Partly the growing French-English tension in our country made historians realize how skilfully King had managed to preserve unity. Also, King's secrets paled in comparison with later revelations about politicians' lives.

Historians obviously change their minds and their judgments. They disagree with each other, too. Some praise St. Laurent for his efficient governing of the country. Others say that almost anyone could have run the country in the prosperous, trouble-free fifties. They point out that St. Laurent

in his last years was depressed, and perhaps somewhat senile. The press in those days guarded secrets about those in power.

This cozy bond broke down in Diefenbaker's and Pearson's times in office. In 1963, Peter Newman, Ottawa editor for *Maclean's*, published *Renegade in Power: The Diefenbaker Years*, an unflattering portrait of Diefenbaker. Dief's supporters denounced the book as character assassination. Newman followed in 1968 with *The Distemper of Our Time*, which revealed behind-the-scenes chaos in Pearson's government.

At the time, Canadians who watched scores of news reports about government scandals probably agreed with Newman that Pearson was incompetent. But were his criticisms fair? Usually historians allow time to pass before making judgments about the accomplishments of leaders. When Pearson announced his retirement, few Canadians polled could recall any of his accomplishments. Decades later, Canadians identify the maple-leaf flag and medicare as their proudest symbols. So how should we judge prime ministers? By their popularity, personality, and personal lives? Or by their policies and principles? And when should we judge them? When they are in office? When their term in office is up, or when the long-term effects of their actions and decisions become clearer?

1. Choose the statement which is not true:

   A   Mackenzie King is a good example of a prime minister about whom public opinion has changed.

   B   He was respected during his time as prime minister.

   C   His private life caused his fall from favour.

   D   He was loved and admired by his people.

2. After his death, when Mackenzie King was criticized, he was described as

   _____

3. By 1997, King was referred to as a "nation-builder" and praised for his

   _____

4. If St. Laurent was not an effective prime minister, why did the country run smoothly during his years as its leader?

   _____

   _____

5. What books did Peter Newman write about prime ministers?

   _____

   _____

6. What two Canadian symbols are associated with Lester B. Pearson?

   _____

7. Who was Canada's longest-serving prime minister?

   _____

8. Choose the expression that is closest in meaning to: "paled in comparison with."

   A   seemed less important when compared with...

   B   seemed more important when compared with ...

   C   became less interesting when compared with...

   D   grew very pale when compared with...

9. Why is the final paragraph made up entirely of questions?

   A   to involve the reader

   B   to find out what information the reader has

   C   to indicate what the reader does not know

   D   to lead the reader to reread the article

1. From the statement, "Also, King's secrets paled in comparison with later revelations about politicians' lives," what conclusion can you draw about the lives of later politicians?

    A They couldn't preserve unity.

    B Their lives involved more scandal and controversy than King's did.

    C Their lives were happier than King's was.

    D Their effectiveness cannot be judged yet.

2. From the statement, "The press in those days guarded secrets about those in power," we can infer that the press

    A have always been powerful

    B had a "tell-all" policy

    C protected leaders to a certain extent

    D have been a nuisance to political leaders

3. What can we infer about the impact of Peter Newman's books on the media?

    _____

    _____

4. From the statement, "Usually historians allow time to pass before making judgments about the accomplishments of leaders," what can we infer about the fairness of Newman's criticism of Pearson's leadership?

    _____

    _____

5. From this article, what can you infer about judging prime ministers while they are still in office?

    _____

    _____

6. Explain in a paragraph what you might infer about when it is best to judge the effectiveness of a prime minister for a country?

    _____

    _____

    _____

    _____

    _____

    _____

    _____

1. Explain what is meant by the statement, "he was not loved, but he was respected."

    _____

    _____

    _____

2. To what does "the rehabilitation of King" refer?

    _____

    _____

3. Why is *Maclean's* in italics?

    _____

4. What does the author mean by the statement, "this cozy bond broke down in Diefenbaker's and Pearson's times in office"?

    _____

    _____

    _____

5. Explain what is meant by "character assassination."

    _____

    _____

    _____

6. Explain in a paragraph what is meant by the statement, "Canadians identify the maple-leaf flag and medicare as their proudest symbols."

    _____

    _____

    _____

    _____

    _____

    _____

    _____

    _____

1. Give two reasons for the change in opinion about Mackenzie King as a prime minister (from after his death to 1997).

   _____

   _____

   _____

2. Explain why St. Laurent's personal condition during his last years in power was not well known.

   _____

   _____

   _____

3. Explain the probable impact of Peter Newman's book on Pearson's reputation at the time.

   _____

   _____

   _____

4. Why could few Canadians recall any of Pearson's accomplishments when he retired?

   _____

   _____

   _____

5. Explain in a paragraph why we should probably evaluate prime ministers "only when the long-term effects of their actions and decisions become clearer."

   _____

   _____

   _____

   _____

   _____

   _____

   _____

   _____

   _____

   _____

Writing

Purpose and audience

Remember that you are writing these samples to prove your ability to communicate ideas clearly and accurately, and that your audience in each case is an adult. Therefore, your language should be formal enough to reflect your purpose and your audience. This means that you will need to choose your words carefully, avoid slang expressions, and write in complete, grammatical sentences. Write to create a good impression and with the care that you would take if you were applying for a job!

Length

The length of the piece of writing expected should be indicated by the space provided or in the instructions. Check to be sure that you have written enough to give a good indication of your writing ability. Answers that are too short will not be marked but will fail on the basis of length.

Paragraphs

A carefully constructed paragraph should include five to seven sentences, in the following usual order:

i)   a clear topic sentence, which introduces your paragraph;

ii) three or four elaborative sentences of further explanation, supporting your topic sentence with details and examples, in order of importance, or reverse order; and

iii) a concluding sentence to give a sense of completeness, which may refer back to the topic sentence.

Where you are asked for more than one paragraph, show clear paragraph divisions.

Instructions

Read over the instructions for each piece of writing and underline what you are asked for. Be sure that you are answering the question or giving information that is required. Don't drift away with your own opinion. Give your opinion only when requested to do so.

Writing Skills to Be Tested

• **Writing a summary**

• **Writing to express an opinion**

• **Writing a news report**

• **Writing an information paragraph**

Tips!

Remember:
• Take time to read the instructions carefully and then *follow* them!
• Your language reflects your audience.
• Stay on topic, create a logical order, and "introduce, prove, conclude."
• Write to an appropriate length and always show clear paragraph divisions.

Writing a Summary

A **summary** is a condensed and shorter version of a passage.

The following suggestions will help you to write a **summary**:

• Underline, circle, or highlight the most important ideas in the text.

• Read the passage carefully to determine the main idea.

• Select the most important supporting details to include.

• You will definitely need to leave out information from the original. You might choose to do this by eliminating any information which is not absolutely essential to understanding the main idea. You may also leave out specific examples, by grouping them together, for example, or choose the best example to represent all of them.

• Write your summary smoothly, so that the reader understands from your words, rather than having to read the original piece. Use good connecting words and ideas to show transitions.

• Proofread to eliminate errors, and write in your neatest handwriting for legibility.

Read the article "The Metric System (Sort Of)," on the following page, and write a summary of 50–100 words, including the main idea and at least three details which support it.

_____

_____

_____

_____

_____

_____

_____

_____

_____

_____

_____

The Metric System (Sort Of)

Canada was declared a metric nation in 1971, and after 2.8 decades, it's safe to say that we're as metric as we're going to get. At first the two systems, metric and imperial, battled it out—the metricists seized the road signs and thermostats, while the stubborn imperialists refused to buy anything that wasn't measured out according to some body part. You may recall extremists in Ottawa driving all the way to Carleton Place, a distance of sixty-three kilometres, to fill up at a service station that still sold gasoline in gallons. But that's all over now. Resistance and insistence proved equally futile.

Purists on both sides have lamented the resulting mish-mash, failing to see that what we have now is a system that's uniquely Canadian. By combining the more sensible features of the metric system, or SI (for *Système international d'unités*), with some long-cherished aspects of the imperial system, we've come up with a seamless hybrid that makes perfect sense to us all. Let's call it simperial. Like franglais and "Progressive Conservative," simperial is the ideal Canadian compromise.

For example, the other day I asked directions to an auction sale: "Drive ten kilometres down this road," I was told, "and you'll see a barn about two hundred feet in from the highway." That's simperial. Only in Canada can a river be half a mile wide and thirty metres deep. At building supply yards, you can buy 100 square metres of shingles and a box of three-quarter-inch roofing nails to hold them down. When I ask my daughter, who is fourteen and has been raised metric, how tall she is, she says "Five four." What's the temperature outside? "Plus three." Simperial.

In our quiet, peacekeeping way, we took the best features from each extreme and consigned the rest to oblivion. Simperial simply makes more sense than either of its two feeder systems. Nobody's feet should be size forty-two anything. But at the same time, zero degrees, not thirty-two, is obviously the temperature at which water should freeze; if anyone knows that, it's us.

Writing to Express an Opinion

Your assigned task will be to write a series of paragraphs expressing an **opinion** on a topic.

Here are several suggestions to help you to express your **opinion** clearly:

- Divide your writing into **paragraphs** of five to seven sentences.

  – In your introductory paragraph, you need to include a clear statement of your opinion. You do not need to say "I think that" or "I believe that," because the entire essay is your opinion.

  – You do need to state clearly what you think or believe should happen; for example, if you are writing about the benefits of volunteer experience for teenagers, you need to outline (perhaps even number) the benefits clearly. This means explaining **why**, as well as **what**.

  Not simply: Volunteering is good for teenagers to do.

  But instead: Teenagers who volunteer have a chance to learn about their community and increase their social skills at the same time.

- Make a **plan** before you write. This should only take a *few* minutes but it will help you to organize your ideas. You may add to the plan as you write. Following it will definitely help you to keep on track, and the few minutes you spend writing it is an investment in your results.

  Example: Teenagers and volunteering

  1. good way to get experience and references
  2. meet people, learn, and develop social skills
  3. give to the community and help teenagers' reputation

- Avoid talking only in general terms; give **examples** of what you are saying, and give **evidence** to support your opinion.

- Your paragraphs should **flow** logically from one to the next with connecting ideas and transition words, such as "on the other hand," or "as well as...." Be sure that your ideas are clearly explained so that the reader can understand your opinion.

- In your final paragraph, try to **conclude** your thoughts, even by summarizing the main points of your argument. Leave the reader with a positive thought at the end.

- **Proofread**, of course, and write neatly and legibly.

- Give your work a **title** that shows your creativity and thoughtfulness.

Practise!

Write a series of paragraphs (a minimum of three paragraphs of about five to seven sentences each) expressing your opinion on this topic:
Volunteering is a good experience for teenagers.

Be sure to remember to show clear divisions between paragraphs, and organize your ideas so that you have a main idea with examples and evidence to support your opinion.

_____

_____

_____

_____

_____

_____

_____

_____

_____

_____

_____

_____

_____

_____

_____

_____

_____

_____

_____

_____

_____

_____

_____

_____

_____

_____

_____

_____

_____

Writing a News Report

A **news report** is written to inform people of what is happening. It begins with a **lead**—an introductory section that gives the most important information about the story, answering most or all of the **W5 + H** questions:

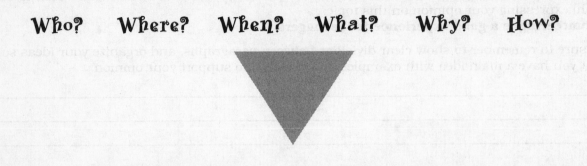

After the lead comes the **body** of the news report. It provides details that build on the facts given in the lead. Toward the end of the report, the information may be less interesting and important. This is the **inverted pyramid style** of writing. A news report is completed by a **headline** that attracts the reader's attention and informs the reader of the topic.

Here are some suggestions that will help you write an effective **news report**:

- Use **inverted pyramid style**: This means that most factual information is given in the first paragraph or two. This includes the **who**, **where**, **when**, **what**, **why**, and **how** of the event. The rest of the article, after this factual information is given, is made up of supporting details, quotations, and background information to help the reader understand more about what happened.

- **Paragraphs** in news reporting are usually one or two sentences long. They are much shorter than the paragraphs you would normally be writing of five to seven sentences.

- You may use **quotations** from people who were at the scene, or you may use the **opinions** of experts on the subject. (Of course, for this report, you will have to create these.) This gives your article more credibility since it is not just one reporter's opinion on what happened.

- Use your best **journalistic style**, and pretend that you are writing for a real newspaper. Use connecting words and good transitions between sentences and between paragraphs.

- **Proofread** and write legibly! Your goal is for your audience to understand what happened.

Practise!

Write a news report based on the following photograph and headline. Write this report as if you were in the audience on the day of this famous address. Indicate your feelings about what King has said and tell how his powerful address affected and inspired the crowd. You will have to make up most of the facts that you include, but because this speech was an important moment in our history, you may already know of some of the details around the civil rights movement. You may include quotations from witnesses or experts (also made up). Create your own headline if you prefer.

I have a dream

Until the 1960s, African-Americans did not have equal rights in all parts of the United States. The civil rights movement, led by Martin Luther King, Jr., demanded those rights. On the steps of the Lincoln Memorial, August 28, 1963, King addressed a massive rally of the civil rights movement. The U.S. Civil Rights Act became law in 1964, and King's speech became a cry for civil rights all around the world.

(Continued on next page)

Practise!

_____
_____
_____
_____
_____
_____
_____
_____
_____
_____
_____
_____
_____

Writing an Information Paragraph

The purpose of an **information paragraph** is to convey important information to a reader. To accomplish this, it must be clear, carefully organized, and accurate. This type of writing is often used to inform or educate people about issues, and might be seen, for example, in a brochure on a health-related topic. It is also the type of writing that you will find in an encyclopedia. It involves selecting relevant and important details from a research source and writing them in a smooth, informative paragraph.

Here are some suggestions that will help you to write an effective **information paragraph**:

• Make **decisions about what to include**, since there is too much information and not all of it is necessary. To do this, read through the sample and choose several (at least five) main details that seem most important.

• Write a **topic sentence** in which the main idea is clearly expressed. You may choose part or all of your topic sentence from the information provided. Make every word count, and delete unnecessary information.

• Be certain that your sentences relate well to one another with the use of transition words and **logical order** of ideas.

• **Write** legibly and **proofread** carefully so that your work is clear.

• It is always effective to add a title that interests the reader and reveals a little information about the focus of your writing. **Avoid boring titles!**

Practise!

Write an information paragraph based on your selection of important aspects from the sample below and the one on page 18. Write this paragraph as if your purpose is to tie together smoothly important facts and ideas, so that the reader will have an accurate understanding of the subject. Your paragraph should be five to seven sentences long and should indicate careful organization with a topic sentence, supporting ideas, and a concluding sentence. Be sure to include a minimum of five relevant details.

Thelma Chalifoux, Senator

• Thelma Chalifoux is the first Aboriginal woman in Canada to become a senator

• she was born in Alberta, with roots in the Métis community for many generations

• she was raised among relatives who worked for the rights of the Métis

• she began her career as a field worker, first with the Métis Association of Alberta

• then she worked with an agency called the Company of Young Canadians

• she travelled through Northern Alberta, helping to improve Métis living conditions

• she also helped community members work to establish vocational centres and support groups

• she received a National Aboriginal Achievement Award

• when appointed to the Senate, she found that her fellow senators and the general public knew very little about Aboriginal peoples

• she has used her position to educate Canadians about the different languages, cultures, and histories of Aboriginal Nations in Canada

• she is a member of the Senate Standing Committee of Aboriginal Peoples

• she also speaks on behalf of the French communities of Northern Alberta, which are largely unknown to the rest of the country

• "If you forget where you come from, then you've lost sight of what you're supposed to be doing," says Chalifoux

• her position gives her the power to be able to help more people and make real changes

_____

_____

_____

_____

_____

_____

_____

_____

_____

Practise!

Technology and the Northern Cod

- in 1497, John Cabot returned to England raving about the fish that were so plentiful that they slowed the progress of his boats
- although this was exaggerated, the cod fishery has shaped the lives of Atlantic Canadians
- it has been part of our economy, our culture, our diet, and even our songs
- overfishing is seen as the main problem
- technological change allowed the overfishing
- navigational advances included radar, echo sounders, and lorans
- with these tools, fishers could locate good fishing sites
- they could also go farther from shore to locate new fish stocks
- previously, fishers had to rely on their fishing experience to locate fish
- new technology meant that fishers did not need the skills of experience
- those with less experience, but the right equipment, could catch more fish
- an even bigger factor was the factory-freezer trawler
- these vessels could hold from 2000 to 4000 tonnes of fish
- one Russian ship was known to carry as much as 8000 tonnes
- these trawlers became the vacuum cleaners of the sea
- between the mid-1950s and mid-1960s the total catch of northern cod almost tripled
- although fish stocks were going down, operators were able to catch even more fish
- by 1978 the catch had dropped dramatically
- the government closed the fishery in 1992, why not sooner?
- there were no accurate ways to estimate how many fish were in the ocean
- the technology of resource management lagged behind fish-catching technology
- fish stocks were overestimated for many years
- cod stocks were so low that many wondered if the species would survive

_____

_____

_____

_____

_____

_____

_____

_____

_____

_____

_____

Sample Reading and Writing Tasks

History Article

Note: *The Great Depression occurred during the 1930s, following the stock market crash of 1929. It was a time of hardship, food rationing, and mass unemployment for most people in North America.*

Life in the Depression

While some wealthy and middle-class Canadians with secure jobs noticed little change in their lifestyle, many people suffered terribly. Thousands were fired from their jobs, and hundreds of businesses failed. People were evicted from their homes because they couldn't afford to pay rent. Farmers on the Prairies watched their livelihood blow away on the wind. Thousands existed on "pogey"—relief payments that brought shame to those who had no alternative.

Canadians valued self-reliance. They thought it shameful to accept government assistance. One Winnipeg man returned home to discover that his wife who had been living on relief, had drowned their son, strangled their daughter, and poisoned herself. The note she left said, "I owe the drugstore 44 cents. Farewell."

For those willing to swallow their pride, the government did not make getting relief any easier. People had to wait in line for hours and then publicly declare their failure and swear that they did not own anything of value. They had to be under eviction notice, and to have had their water and electricity cut off. If they met these requirements, they received vouchers that could be used to buy food. The value of these vouchers depended on where they lived. In Ontario, some received as much as $8.07 a week during the winter. In New Brunswick, most got only $1.67. The vouchers were never enough, and they could never be obtained without humiliation.

Private charities also helped those who were desperate, providing used clothing and meals. Soup kitchens were set up to help the hungry and the homeless. At the same time, many municipalities were afraid of the poor, and harassed them so that they would leave their towns.

Single men, with no families to keep them at home, moved from one place to another in search of work. Penniless, they travelled across the country by "hopping" freight trains. Those who could not manage to avoid the railway guards and get inside a car sometimes rode on the roof or clung to the rods underneath the train.

Canadians who had been at a disadvantage when times were good suffered even more during the Great Depression. For women, there were no jobs other than domestic work. Some domestics worked for just a few dollars a week, and some worked for room and board only. Aboriginal families on relief got only $5 a month. They were expected to "live off the land," even though conditions on the reserves were so poor that they had been unable to do so for decades. In 1931, the government put a complete stop to immigration.

History Article: *Life in the Depression*

1. Canadian people valued "self-reliance." This means that

   A   they were desperate and asked for government relief

   B   they demanded better jobs from the government

   C   they didn't want to rely on the government for relief

   D   they didn't trust the government

2. Single men "hopped" freight trains hoping to

   A   travel

   B   find work

   C   find food

   D   escape bill payments

3. Why is the word "pogey" in quotation marks?

   _____

   _____

4. Why did people find relief payments humiliating?

   _____

   _____

   _____

5. Explain why there was a need for private charities.

   _____

   _____

   _____

   _____

   _____

6. For what possible reasons would municipalities have been afraid of the poor?

   _____

   _____

   _____

   _____

   _____

   _____

Mathematics Article

The End of the Century, 1984–1999: A Changing Nation

What has been the impact of various forces of change in Canada since the early 1980s? Review the data below to understand some of the ways in which our society has changed.

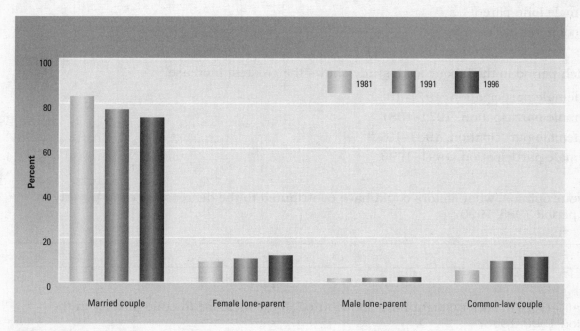

Families by family structure, Canada, 1981, 1991, and 1996

Year	Male participation rate	Female participation rate
1971	76.4%	39.9%
1981	78.5	52.1
1991	76.5	59.7
1996	72.4	57.6

Labour force participation rates (for percentage of population over 15 years of age), Canada, 1971–1996

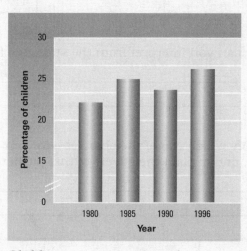

Child poverty rates, Canada, 1980–1996

Mathematics Article: *A Changing Nation: Interpreting Statistical Data*

1. Which family structure has changed the most since 1981?

   A   married couple
   B   female lone-parent
   C   male lone-parent
   D   common-law couple

2. Which period in the labour force study shows the greatest increase?

   A   female participation, 1971–1981
   B   male participation, 1971–1981
   C   female participation, 1981–1991
   D   male participation, 1991–1996

3. In your opinion, what factors could have contributed to the decrease in child poverty in the period 1985–1990?

   _____

   _____

4. What factors in society might have contributed to the increase in child poverty in the period 1990–1996?

   _____

   _____

5. What can you interpret from the statistics for male lone-parent families since 1981?

   _____

   _____

6. Identify which one of the changes—in your opinion—has affected Canadian society the most, and explain the effects of this particular social trend.

   _____

   _____

   _____

   _____

   _____

   _____

   _____

   _____

Should We Protect Canadian Culture?

Americans who are in the business of exporting American culture disagree with any attempts to protect and enhance Canadian culture. They believe that cultural industries such as television, movies, and music are just that—industries or businesses in which to make money. The Americans have been very successful in exporting their cultural products around the world, and want to continue this trend.

Most other countries, including Canada, feel that culture is much more than a business. They feel it is a critical part of their identity as a nation, and American cultural exports are a threat to this identity. As a result, they have decided to do what they can to protect their culture. For example, France tries to stop English words like microcomputer and slamdunk—most of which come from the United States—from being adopted into the French language. In another case, Iran has banned satellite dishes to try to keep American television and movies out. The attitudes of young Canadians like yourself over the next half century will determine the direction that Canada's culture will take.

Movies

Every year, the Genie awards are presented to Canada's outstanding movies. Most Canadians look at the list of winners and ask, "Why haven't I heard of most of these movies?" The reason that people have not heard of these Canadian movies has nothing to do with the quality of the movies. Rather, it is related to the way in which movies are distributed. Canadian movies rarely are shown in large theatres owned by companies like Famous Players and Cineplex-Odeon. These companies are huge American companies which are most interested in showing American movies with big-name stars and continent-wide advertising.

Popular Music

Perhaps in no other cultural field have Canadians been as successful as they have been in popular music. You can probably name several Canadian performers or groups who have a national and even an international appeal. For example, in 1998, two of the ten best-selling CDs in Canada featured Canadian artists.

This situation has not occurred by accident however. Obviously, a lot of very talented musicians and singers live in Canada, but so do many talented people in television, films, and radio. The difference involves an effective set of government regulations that requires Canadian radio stations to play a certain percentage of Canadian music. These rules help Canadian artists to land recording contracts and then encourages their music to have exposure on the air. Without these rules, the Canadian music industry would not be as healthy as it is today.

Media Article: *Should We Protect Canadian Culture?*

1. How do most other countries regard American cultural exports?

   A   as a helpful source of marketing ideas

   B   as a way of maintaining positive international relations

   C   as a way of keeping up to date with North America

   D   as a threat to their cultural identity

2. Canadian popular musical performers have experienced success in Canada because

   A   a lot of talented musicians and singers live in Canada

   B   there are rules requiring Canadian radio to play a percentage of Canadian music

   C   there are rules prohibiting the music of other countries, specifically the United States

   D   the Canadian music industry is healthy

3. Explain why most Canadians have not heard of many Canadian movies.

   _____

   _____

4. Explain the differences in regulations between the Canadian movie industry and the Canadian music industry.

   _____

   _____

   _____

   _____

   _____

5. What argument do American cultural exporters use against any attempts to protect Canadian culture?

   _____

   _____

6. Do you agree with the steps taken by France or Iran? Explain your opinion in a paragraph.

   _____

   _____

   _____

   _____

   _____

   _____

   _____

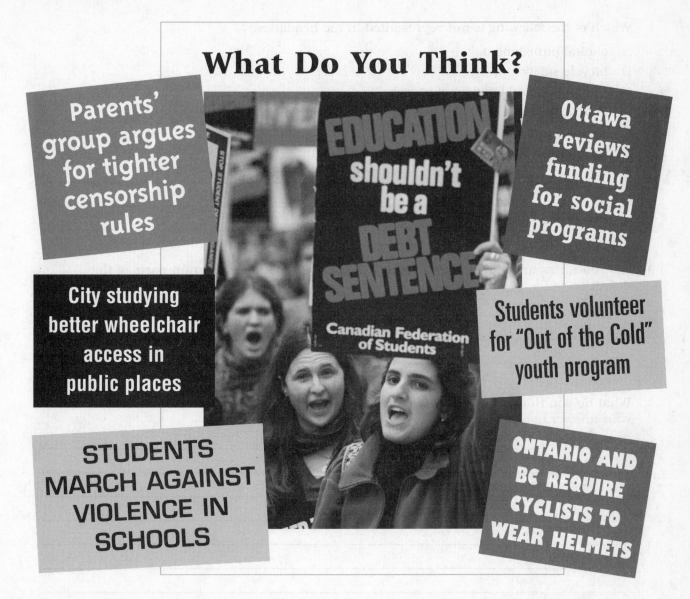

What Do You Think?

Parents' group argues for tighter censorship rules

Ottawa reviews funding for social programs

EDUCATION shouldn't be a DEBT SENTENCE
Canadian Federation of Students

City studying better wheelchair access in public places

Students volunteer for "Out of the Cold" youth program

STUDENTS MARCH AGAINST VIOLENCE IN SCHOOLS

ONTARIO AND BC REQUIRE CYCLISTS TO WEAR HELMETS

When you look at headlines like these, you can see that in today's world, we face some difficult issues. Citizenship is about how we choose to respond to these issues. It is about the decisions we make and the actions we take to influence the ways in which our communities change and develop.

Responsible citizenship means having the knowledge to understand the issues we face. It also means using that knowledge to make effective decisions. Are you ready to meet the challenges of the twenty-first century? To what extent will you, as a citizen, participate in shaping your future?

Civics Article: *What Do You Think?*

1. Which of the following is **not** represented in the headlines:

    A   capital punishment
    B   bicycle safety
    C   censorship and freedom of speech
    D   education costs

2. Explain the pun used in the headline on education.

    _____

    _____

    _____

3. How does this article define citizenship? Quote the two most important parts of the definition.

    _____

    _____

    _____

4. What do you think are the most important characteristics of a responsible citizen? Explain your answer in a paragraph.

    _____

    _____

    _____

    _____

    _____

    _____

5. Do you feel you are primarily a citizen of your community, of your country, or of the world? Explain your answer in a paragraph.

    _____

    _____

    _____

    _____

    _____

    _____

Science Article

Life in a Greenhouse

At some time in your life, you may have had the experience of sitting in a car on a sunny day in the winter with the engine turned off. In spite of the cold temperature outside, the car's interior was getting hot. You may even have had to open a window to cool down the car. What you experienced is called the **greenhouse effect** (Fig. 35-4). A similar situation exists in the Earth's atmosphere, although obviously no window is involved (Fig. 35-5). A number of gases, found in the atmosphere, in only tiny amounts, absorb some of the heat before it can escape into space. This greenhouse effect is vital to the existence of life on Earth. If there were no **greenhouse gases**, the average temperature would drop by about 33°C and the Earth would be a cold, lifeless planet more like Mars than the Earth we know. On the other hand, if the amount of greenhouse gas increases, less heat can escape into space and the temperature of the Earth's atmosphere gets higher. The fear is that this is exactly what is happening today—global warming that is being caused by an increase in greenhouse gases as a result of human activities.

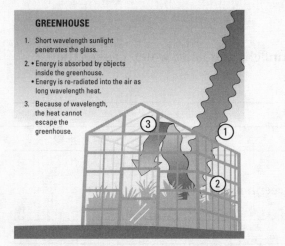

GREENHOUSE

1. Short wavelength sunlight penetrates the glass.

2. • Energy is absorbed by objects inside the greenhouse.
   • Energy is re-radiated into the air as long wavelength heat.

3. Because of wavelength, the heat cannot escape the greenhouse.

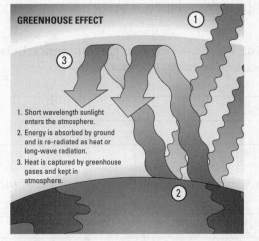

GREENHOUSE EFFECT

1. Short wavelength sunlight enters the atmosphere.

2. Energy is absorbed by ground and is re-radiated as heat or long-wave radiation.

3. Heat is captured by greenhouse gases and kept in atmosphere.

Fig. 35-4 *Sunlight, which is a short wavelength form of radiation, can pass through greenhouse windows where it heats the interior. Heat, which is long wavelength radiation, is given off by the greenhouse interior but cannot pass through the glass. As a result, the greenhouse gets warmer.*

Fig. 35-5 *Without the greenhouse effect, the world would be a frosty place. The problem today is that human activities have increased the extent of the greenhouse effect.*

The main greenhouse gases are **carbon dioxide**, **methane**, nitrous oxide, **halocarbons**, ozone, and water vapour. Except for halocarbons, these chemicals occur naturally, and are responsible for the positive greenhouse effect that allows life to exist. On the other hand, a negative greenhouse effect has occurred due to the enormous growth in the production of greenhouse gases. This growth has several causes including the use of fossil fuels which produce carbon dioxide. Since carbon dioxide is the most important greenhouse gas, this chapter will concentrate on its role in global warming (Fig. 35-6).

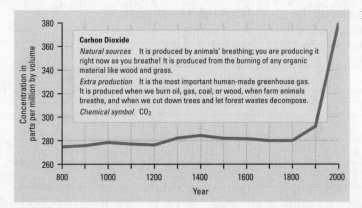

Carbon Dioxide

Natural sources It is produced by animals' breathing; you are producing it right now as you breathe! It is produced from the burning of any organic material like wood and grass.

Extra production It is the most important human-made greenhouse gas. It is produced when we burn oil, gas, coal, or wood, when farm animals breathe, and when we cut down trees and let forest wastes decompose.

Chemical symbol CO_2

Fig. 35-6 *Carbon dioxide is the most important greenhouse gas. When did the amount of carbon dioxide in the atmosphere start to increase? Why?*

Science Article: *Life in a Greenhouse*

1. The **greenhouse effect** is experienced when

    A there are many oxygen-producing plants in a building

    B the sun heats up the Earth, including bodies of water

    C human activities send more heat into space

    D the inside of your car becomes very warm on a cold, sunny day

2. **Global warming** is caused by

    A an increase in greenhouse gases

    B much warmer temperatures in northern climates

    C new textile inventions, such as Thinsulate

    D too much reflective glass used in buildings

3. Using Fig. 35-4, explain the difference between sunlight and heat, which causes the greenhouse to get warmer.

    _____

    _____

    _____

4. Explain what is revealed by Fig. 35-5 about the greenhouse effect.

    _____

    _____

    _____

5. Using Fig. 35-6, explain why the levels of carbon dioxide were relatively stable for centuries, but then suddenly increased tremendously.

    _____

    _____

    _____

    _____

6. In your opinion, what should be done about the greenhouse gases situation?

    _____

    _____

    _____

    _____

    _____

    _____

Good Eats Guide

MAKING THE SWAP	**SMART SWITCHES**
swap . . .	*for . . .*
french fries (360 cal., 18g fat)	**a baked potato** (218 cal., 0g fat)
cheesecake (188 cal., 14g fat)	**angel food cake** (125 cal., 0g fat)
vanilla ice cream (268 cal., 23g fat)	**lowfat frozen yogurt** (200 cal., 4g fat)
a glazed doughnut (192 cal., 13g fat)	**a bagel** (300 cal., 1.4g fat)
chocolate chip cookies (220 cal., 12g fat)	**fig bars** (240 cal., 4g fat)

As reality has it, convenience store cuisine is becoming a staple in many diets these days. Whether it's due to dealing with an empty house after school or trying to fit food into a hectic schedule, many a mini-meal is being made out of snacks and snack food.

The good news is that snacking isn't so bad after all. Snacking can help squelch mid-afternoon munchies (making you less prone to overdo it at mealtime), and it can even help you meet your daily nutritional needs.

Just because you've been given the green light to go grazing doesn't mean you should go crazy. Smart snacking means knowing what to choose and how to make snacking a healthful part of your diet. Here's some help:

1 Choose low-fat and nutrient-rich snacks that'll help you meet your daily nutritional requirements. A banana will help you meet your fruit requirements for the day. Even items like whole-grain crackers or pretzels can help you meet your six to eleven recommended daily servings of carbos.

2 Prepare for snack attacks. Don't give into the high-fat snack selections in your school's vending machines. Instead, pack your own snacks, such as fruit, yogurt, rice cakes, or pretzels.

3 Factor in a little extra fat now and then. You can fit a few fattening snack foods into your diet—it just requires a little extra planning. Eat less fat at other meals to help "budget" in extra fat. For example, drinking non-fat milk instead of lowfat milk and using jam on your toast instead of margarine will make room for two extra teaspoons of fat. (A fatty snack or meal or a day of eating excess fat will not make or break your health. It's how you elect to eat the majority of the time that counts.)

4 Satisfy your sweet tooth in a sensible manner. Some sweets every now and then won't hurt your health. These treats are naturally low in fat: lowfat puddings, fig bars, graham crackers, frozen fruit bars, vanilla wafers, sorbet, and fruit smoothies.

5 Don't fall into snack traps. Beware of snack foods that sound nutritious, but offer little more than fat and calories. Some common culprits: granola bars, microwave popcorn and trail mix (these are often high in fat), and fruit rolls or fruit chews, which rarely have much fruit in them and are often high in sugar.

6 Fibre fill-ups. Foods that are high in fibre help to fill you up. Since most of us only meet half of our fibre needs, it's wise to choose snack foods that are high in fibre. Some good choices: air-popped popcorn or popcorn cakes, fresh fruit or vegetables, whole wheat toast, wheat or bran cereals, lowfat bran muffins.

Health Article: *Good Eats Guide*

1. Which has the most calories?

    A   a bagel

    B   vanilla ice cream

    C   chocolate chip cookies

    D   fig bars

2. Which has the least fat?

    A   a bagel

    B   vanilla ice cream

    C   chocolate chip cookies

    D   fig bars

3. Give three examples from the article of foods that sound nutritious but are really mostly fat and calories.

    _____

4. Give three examples from the article of foods that are high in fibre.

    _____

5. Explain how you can satisfy your sweet tooth in a healthy way.

    _____

    _____

    _____

    _____

    _____

6. Explain how you can "budget" for a little extra fat now and then, and tell whether or not this will hurt you.

    _____

    _____

    _____

    _____

    _____

    _____

    _____

Meet the Owner of a High-Tech Company

Mona El-Tahan is the president and chief executive officer of CORETEC inc., a high-tech company in St. John's, Newfoundland.

Q: Can you briefly describe what you do?

A: My company specializes in developing technology to predict the movement of floating objects at sea through the use of computer models. The floating objects might be vessels, icebergs, oil, or sea ice. The user of our program feeds information into the computer about the wind and ocean currents, the original position of the object, and other details. Then the computer can display where that object will move over a certain period of time. We sell these programs to shipping companies and offshore oil companies.

Q: What is the purpose of the service you provide?

A: Objects like icebergs are major hazards when working at sea. Workers need to know if an iceberg or other object is likely to interfere with their operations, so that they can take appropriate action. They may need to move out of the way or divert the iceberg from its predicted path.

For example, I recently got a request for a model from Hibernia. The main structure is designed to withstand the impact of an iceberg, but the workers still have to protect all the off-loading facilities, the supply boats, and the shuttle tankers. They need to be able to predict what an iceberg is going to do. We also developed a model for Environment Canada to predict what an oil spill will do in the presence of sea ice. There are several other models for predicting the movement of an oil spill in open water, but ours is the only one that considers ice. This is very important in the North Atlantic.

Now we are even serving as advisors to Norwegian and American companies.

Q: How did you get into this kind of work?

A: I did my graduate studies in ocean engineering at Memorial University in Newfoundland. The main topic of my thesis was modelling, or predicting, iceberg drift. My model was the first one developed in North America. It was purely theoretical: I didn't know I could use it in real life. I developed procedures for ice observers, including ways to protect their platforms from icebergs and to tow the icebergs away. I come from Egypt, so some people ask how I ended up working with icebergs. I laugh and tell them that they look much like the Pyramids.

Q: Dealing with icebergs is pretty unusual work. Can you describe any experiences that are especially memorable?

A: I received a call one stormy night around midnight. It was from Mobil, the drilling company working on the Grand Banks. They were in a panic because an iceberg had suddenly been spotted on the horizon. This was shortly after the *Ocean Ranger* disaster, when many people died, and I'm sure that was on their minds. There were over 80 people on board the rig. It was too stormy to send a helicopter to rescue them. I did a forecast in less than a half hour. Luckily it indicated that the iceberg would come close to the drill ship, within about a kilometre, but that it would pass by. Mobil officials asked me how confident I was about my forecast. I answered, "99 percent." When they saw the detailed model,

with information on where the iceberg was and where it was going, they relaxed. They suspended their operations for the night and went to sleep. The next morning they sent a helicopter to see where the iceberg was. It was where I predicted it would be.

Q: Does computer technology play a significant role in your work?

A: Computer technology is really the key. Predicting the behaviour of a floating object that is being acted upon by many forces at the same time requires very sophisticated mathematics with numerous calculations. The computer is programmed to do all this calculating. That's what my models do and they do it fast. If it were not for the computer and the software, the problem could not be solved quickly enough to be of any use as a prediction. It is also essential to display the results in a format that is easy to understand—complete with tables, charts, and maps. This helps people using the information to make the right decisions, even in an emergency.

Q: As well as being an engineer and software specialist, you are also an entrepreneur. Did any of your formal schooling prepare you for that?

A: No. We were not as fortunate as some young people now. I learned everything I know about business through real-life experience. I took some short training courses in project and personnel management, business development, and accounting that were very good. But I believe we never stop learning. You never graduate from life.

Careers Article: *Meet the Owner of a High-Tech Company*

1. For which of the following groups of objects does this company's technology predict the movement?

    A   icebergs and migrating whales

    B   ships, icebergs, oil or sea ice

    C   icebergs and weather systems

    D   international air and sea travel

2. How did Ms. El-Tahan first develop her idea for predicting iceberg drift?

    A   by looking at the pyramids in Egypt

    B   by studying the movement of ships lost at sea

    C   by practising towing icebergs away

    D   by working on her thesis at Memorial University, Newfoundland

3. Explain what happened when Mobil called her about an iceberg.

    _____

    _____

4. How important is computer technology to her work?

    _____

    _____

5. How has technology had an impact on *your* life?

    _____

    _____

    _____

    _____

    _____

6. "But I believe we never stop learning. You never graduate from life." Do you agree or disagree with this statement from the article?

    _____

    _____

    _____

    _____

    _____

    _____

Welfare Was a Life Raft, but Now We Can Swim

Barbara Hager

I remember how we used to count down to welfare-cheque day. I was 12; my brothers were 10 and 5. The cheque would arrive in the mailbox on the first or second of the month. My mother would try to pretend she wasn't anxious, but she would look out the window every five minutes to see if the mailman was on our block.

When it finally arrived, my mother would cash the cheque within the hour, and go directly to Safeway to buy a cart full of food. When we lived in Edmonton, the store was a mile from our house, so we would take a cab home. But in Calgary we lived in subsidized townhouses directly across from the store, so we saved two or three dollars a month in cab fare just by living there.

After shopping for food, she would go to the landlord's apartment to pay the rent, which included utilities, in cash. The only other bill we had, since we didn't have a car or credit cards, was for the telephone. She would buy a money order and take the bus downtown to pay the bill at the head office.

We weren't on welfare intentionally. My father stopped living with us full-time when I was 4 or 5, and from that time on my mother alternated between welfare and low-paying jobs. She tried school a few times—a year of classes that were supposed to lead up to a degree in social work, a course in restaurant management. She worked off and on, too: arranging flowers, waiting tables, painting airplanes, and working on an assembly line at a vegetable cannery. But the money wasn't much more than welfare paid, and she had to worry about who was looking after us, and if we were getting into trouble.

What I learned most about growing up on welfare is that without it my brothers and I might not be where we are today—educated, hard-working, and employed. Though we have never discussed it, I can see a pattern that we have all developed to avoid welfare. We work hard at our marriages because poverty strikes single parents first. We've found ways to learn the skills we need to get jobs that pay more than $8 an hour. My youngest brother is a forester, the other a pilot, and I've worked in professional positions for government for most of the past decade.

Strangely enough, the three of us have all been involved in hiring and training welfare recipients to work for us. Last month I found money to hire one of my summer employees as a part-time arts administrator. She has two young children, and her new part-time salary pays slightly more than her previous net on social assistance. I accidentally overheard her talking to her social worker on the phone after I offered her the job. She proudly informed her that she would be working now, and would probably only need child-care support until the job went full time. When she finished the call, she hung up the phone and let out a sigh that I could hear down the hallway.

We went out for coffee that day to celebrate. She insisted on paying the bill.

Literary Article: *Welfare Was a Life Raft, but Now We Can Swim*

1. In what two cities did the author live as a child?

   _____

2. Why did the child's family need welfare?

   A   father lost his job

   B   mother lost her job

   C   father left

   D   mother left

3. What does "subsidized" mean?

   A   free rent

   B   upscale, suburban housing

   C   rent-controlled

   D   rent adjusted to income

4. Why was it difficult for their mother to keep working?

   _____

   _____

   _____

5. Explain what the author learned about growing up on welfare.

   _____

   _____

   _____

   _____

6. How does the young woman that she hired feel about having a job? Give evidence for your opinion from the essay.

   _____

   _____

   _____

   _____

   _____

   _____

Unit 2

Vocabulary

FOCUS ON: Vocabulary

1. Add **prefixes** and **suffixes** to these root forms to make new words.

   view: _____, _____, _____

   copy: _____, _____, _____

2. For each word, give a **synonym** and an **antonym**.

   tall: _____, _____

   night: _____, _____

3. Write **homonyms** for these words. Check that your homonyms are spelled correctly.

   their: _____   guessed: _____

   plain: _____   presents: _____

4. What do these **idioms** mean?

   catch red-handed: _____

   cut loose: _____

   rain cats and dogs: _____

   toe the line: _____

5. What do these **acronyms** stand for?

   laser: _____

   scuba: _____

   NASA: _____

6. Give the full words for these **abbreviations**.

   Wed.: _____   Aug.: _____

   govt.: _____   apt.: _____

7. Rewrite this **informal** English sentence in **formal** English.
   Well, you see, if you just go up the road a ways and turn at the old barn, you'll get there alright.

   _____

   _____

8. Rewrite this sentence in **informal** English.
   The best way to do this job is to try, Mr. Calaban.

   _____

Vocabulary

A **prefix** is a word part added to the beginning of a word. Some prefixes are:

anti- de- semi- dis- hyper-

mid- mis- out- over- sub- trans-

> A **prefix** can change the meaning of a **root form**. Sometimes, it makes it the opposite meaning: **happy** to **unhappy**.

1. Use the **prefixes** above to create new words. Add them to these **root forms**. Check your words in a dictionary to make sure they are correct terms.

   freeze: _____   active: _____   town: _____

   code: _____   conductor: _____   distance: _____

   fortune: _____   eat: _____   plant: _____

   cover: _____   way: _____   marine: _____

2. Some **prefixes** use **hyphens** when they are added to **root forms**: **great-grandfather**. Use this rule as you add these prefixes to the following root forms: **self- all-** Check your words in a dictionary to make sure they are correct terms.

   taught: _____   knowing: _____

3. A common prefix is **pre-**. Make as many words as you can by adding this prefix to root forms. Check your words in a dictionary.

   _____

   _____

   _____

   _____

   _____

4. Another common prefix is **un-**. Make as many words as you can by adding this prefix to root forms. Check your words in a dictionary.

   _____

   _____

   _____

   _____

5. Select a few of the **prefixed words** from this page. Use them in two sentences. Underline the words that are prefixed in your sentences.

   (a) _____

   (b) _____

▶ *Make a list of prefixed words you see as you read material. Use these words in your writings.*

Vocabulary

A **suffix** is a word part added to the end of a word. Some suffixes are:

-able -ance -ate -dom -ful -ics -less -like -tion -ward -y

> Adding **suffixes** to **root forms** changes the meanings of the words. As you add suffixes, watch the spelling of the new words. Some letters may need to be changed. Check your words in a dictionary to be sure.

1. Use the **suffixes** above to create new words. Add them to these **root forms**. Check your words in a dictionary to make sure they are correct terms.

    perish: _____   resist: _____   king: _____

    wonder: _____   help: _____   reject: _____

    back: _____   life: _____   storm: _____

    gymnast: _____   hyphen: _____   beauty: _____

2. Some **suffixes** use a **hyphen** when they are added to **root forms**: **president-elect**. Use this rule as you add these suffixes to the following root forms: **-free**, **-elect**. Check your words in a dictionary. Use each word you create in a sentence to show its meaning.

    home: _____   government: _____

    _____

    _____

    _____

3. A common suffix is **-ness**. Make as many words as you can by adding this suffix to root forms. Check your words in a dictionary.

    _____

    _____

    _____

    _____

4. A **suffix** that means *state of being* or *part of a group* is **-hood**, such as **childhood** (state of being a child). Add this suffix to these root forms to make new words. Tell what each word means.

    man: _____ : _____

    sister: _____ : _____

    woman: _____ : _____

5. Select several **suffixed words** from this page. Use them in two sentences that show their meanings.

    (a) _____

    _____

    (b) _____

> *Make a list of suffixed words you see as you read material. Use these words in your writing.*

Vocabulary

Synonyms are words that mean the same, or almost the same. They are used when a writer wants a better or different word, but wants to keep the same, basic meaning. Look at this example.

correct: *synonyms* accurate, exact, precise, proper, right.

Each one of the synonyms offers a slightly different perspective on the word correct. They all mean **correct**.

1. Use the **synonyms** for **correct** to complete these sentences. Think about your choice of synonym before you use it. Make sure it fits the context best.

> The **context** is the **meaning** of the sentence. One synonym of **correct** will fit a particular sentence better than another. Read the sentence first before deciding which synonym to use.

   (a) The computer gave an _____ number of errors in the piece.

   (b) We need a _____ count of these boxes.

   (c) What is the _____ answer to the question?

   (d) Always use the _____ gasoline for your car.

2. Synonyms can be found in a **thesaurus**. Use a thesaurus to find synonyms for these words.

   humour: _____

   display: _____

   part: _____

   vacation: _____

3. **Antonyms** are words that are opposite in meaning: **day–night**; **yesterday–tomorrow**. Write an antonym for each of these words. Check your words in a thesaurus.

   real: _____   tallest: _____   proceed: _____

   horizontal: _____   appear: _____   noisy: _____

   eager: _____   fierce: _____   complex: _____

   ignite: _____   tame: _____   winner: _____

4. Complete these sentences with **antonyms** of the **boldfaced** words.

   (a) We wanted a **real** wooden table, but got one made out of _____ materials instead.

   (b) It's **quiet** now, but soon this room will be _____ with party-goers.

   (c) Keep it **simple**; don't get _____.

   (d) This is the **least** we can do after you gave us _____ of the credit.

▶ *Create a list of interesting synonyms for the word "said," which you could use in a story.*

Vocabulary

Homonyms are words that sound the same but have different spellings and meanings:

claws, clause; grown, groan; phase, faze.

> **Homonyms** are also known as **homophones**. They have the same sounds, but have different meanings.

1. Write a **homonym** for each of these words. Check your spellings in a dictionary.

    guilt: _____   flower: _____   pact: _____

    taught: _____   magnet: _____   wood: _____

    threw: _____   course: _____   band: _____

2. Some **homonyms** can be in groups of three: **to, too, two**. Give homonyms in groups of three for these words. Check your words in a dictionary.

    freeze: _____, _____

    there: _____, _____

    prays: _____, _____

    right: _____, _____

    vane: _____, _____

3. Use **homonyms** of the **boldfaced** words to complete these sentences.

    (a) There was **undue** alarm in trying to _____ the ropes.

    (b) Everybody **waits** to use the _____.

    (c) She **rode** a camel on a dirt _____ in the desert.

    (d) I don't have enough **cash** to buy more _____ for my computer!

    (e) Who **knew** the _____ would escape from the zoo?

4. Select four **homonym pairs** or **groups** from this page. Use them in four sentences that show their meanings.

    (a) _____

    _____

    (b) _____

    _____

    (c) _____

    _____

    (d) _____

    _____

> ▶ *Find examples of words that are spelled the same, but have different pronunciations: **read, read.** Use these words in your writing to add interest.*

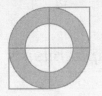

Vocabulary

An **idiom** is an expression whose meaning is not predictable from the usual meanings of the words that make it up. For example, **lend a hand** means **help**. Idioms can enhance your writing. For example, look at these two sentences.

> **Idioms** are particular to the language. They are difficult to translate, since their meanings are only understood by the people who understand the particular language. Idioms should be used only occasionally.

(a) I hope I don't **fail** in my new job.   (b) I hope I don't **fall flat on my face** in my new job.

Sentence (a) tells you what the writer hopes won't happen. Sentence (b) says the same thing, but with more expression or *flavour*.

1. Write what you think each of these **idioms** means.

    sweat of one's brow: _____

    catch red-handed: _____

    break a leg: _____

    for the birds: _____

2. For each of the **idioms** in Activity #1, write a sentence to show its meaning.

    (a) _____

    _____

    (b) _____

    _____

    (c) _____

    _____

    (d) _____

    _____

    (e) _____

    _____

3. Use the following **idioms** in sentences to show their meanings. Try to put your sentences together into a paragraph on one topic.

    wipe the slate clean   up to no good   make up for   here and now   from top to toe

    _____

    _____

    _____

    _____

    _____

 Make a list of interesting idioms that do not mean exactly what they say. Use them in your writings in such a way that the reader understands their meanings from context.

Vocabulary

A **euphemism** is a soft or mild term used in place of a harsh or proper term. For example, to **pass on** is a euphemism for **die**. A workers' **strike** might be called a **withdrawal of services**. Euphemisms are used to tone down the meaning of a word or phrase. They are also usually vague (not clear) in meaning.

> **Euphemisms** appear whenever the speaker (or writer) wants to be vague or not as clear as can be. They should be used sparingly.

1. Match the euphemisms in the box with the actual terms below.

   sanitary engineer   vertically challenged   gathering of individuals insufficient funds

   broke: _____   short: _____

   janitor: _____   crowd: _____

2. Match the following euphemisms with the terms below.

   vocalize loudly   illegally enter the premises   poorly thought-through concept deliriously well-executed ball manoeuvre   without usage   destruction beyond a doubt

   slam, dunk: _____

   crash: _____

   break and enter: _____

   yell: _____

   stupid idea: _____

   broken: _____

3. Use five of the six euphemisms in Activity #2 in sentences to show their meanings.

   (a) _____

   _____

   (b) _____

   _____

   (c) _____

   _____

   (d) _____

   _____

   (e) _____

   _____

Create euphemisms for terms you find in everyday reading. You may also want to look for examples of euphemisms in areas such as words from members of a government.

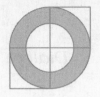

Vocabulary

Clichés are expressions used in place of words to add *flavour* to writings.

However, these expressions are often so overused that they become trite when spoken or written. Look at these examples of clichés.

> **Clichés** and **proverbs** are not very original. Once they are used by a speaker, the listener (or reader) usually knows what is being really said. They are overworked expressions. Use them sparingly.

He's **at death's door.** (He's dying.)

He got caught by the **long arm of the law.** (He got caught by the police.)

1. Write what you think these **clichés** mean.

   beat about the bush: _____

   few and far between: _____

   no rhyme nor reason: _____

2. Use these **clichés** in sentences to show their meanings.

   last but not least: _____

   _____

   the bottom line: _____

   _____

   as luck would have it: _____

   _____

3. Another form of expression is a **proverb**. It is similar to a cliché in that it is often overused. A proverb is an old saying that expresses a general truth. It is used to give a meaning to something being talked or written about. For example, the proverb **All is fair in love and war** means **Anything is acceptable**. Write what you think these proverbs mean.

   You can lead a horse to water, but you can't make him drink.

   _____

   The early bird gets the worm.

   _____

   You let the cat out of the bag.

   _____

4. Write a sentence using one of the **proverbs** in Activity #3.

   _____

   _____

 Listen as people talk. Notice how many clichés or proverbs are used in daily conversation. Make a list of some of the more common clichés and proverbs.

Vocabulary

A **dialect** is a collection of words specific to a part of a country, or the country as a whole.

It can also be the speech patterns of a particular ethnic group, such as a French dialect.

Look at these examples of Canadian dialect:

There is a **wind-chill factor** of –35°C today.

Let's **have a visit** to the East Town Mall.

> Use a **dialectal word** or **term** if it will add a certain *flavour* to your writing. Don't overuse dialect as it might not be understood by all of your readers.

1. Use these examples of Canadian **dialect** in sentences.

   get awake: _____

   _____

   no more I don't: _____

   _____

   happy as a clam at high tide: _____

   _____

2. A much-used Canadian dialectal word is **eh**. Make a list of other Canadian **dialectal words** you know.

   _____

   _____

   _____

   _____

   _____

3. Write a paragraph using some of the **dialectal words** in Activities #1 and #2. Add some new ones that you can think of as well.

   _____

   _____

   _____

   _____

   _____

   _____

   _____

Dialectal words and expressions are frequently used in our everyday speech. Listen to people talk. Determine if what you are hearing are really dialectal words or not. Add these words to a list of dialectal terms.

Vocabulary

Abbreviations and Acronyms

Abbreviations are shortened forms of words. The words are shortened and periods are used to complete the abbreviation: **Inc.** for **Incorporated**. Here are other forms of abbreviations:

- **suspensions:** shortened forms where the middle of the word has been dropped. Periods are usually used: **Cdn.** for **Canadian**

- **acronyms:** shortened forms that use the first letter or initial letters in each word to form a term pronounced as a word: **laser** for **l**ight **a**mplification by **s**timulated **e**mission or **r**adiation

- **initialisms:** similar to acronyms, but spoken letter by letter: **CBC** for **C**anadian **B**roadcasting **C**orporation. Periods are sometimes used in the initialism: **P.S.** for **p**ost **s**cript.

- **postal codes:** in Canada, names of provinces are abbreviated to two letters: **SK** for **Saskatchewan**. No periods are used.

1. Write the long form for each of these **abbreviations**.

    Feb. _____   Wed. _____   ON _____

    adj. _____   Corp. _____   Mr. _____

    tel. no. _____   Ave. _____   mtn. _____

2. Write an **acronym** for each of these groups of words.

    radio directing and ranging: _____   Canadian deuterium uranium: _____

    National Aeronautics Space Administration: _____

    self–contained underwater breathing apparatus: _____

    Organization of Petroleum Exporting Countries: _____

    General Agreement on Tariffs and Trade: _____

3. Write **abbreviations** for these groups of words.

    revolutions per minute: _____   I owe you: _____

    bacon, lettuce, tomato: _____   world-wide web: _____

    very important person: _____   television: _____

4. Rewrite these sentences substituting the **abbreviated forms** with their **longer forms**. Use a dictionary to help you with difficult abbreviations.

    (a) I want this package sent COD to Rankin Rd. by Sun.

    _____

    (b) Last Mar., we visited the US, in particular LA, and got caught on the Van Nuys Frwy.

    _____

 Try writing a piece that uses mostly abbreviations and acronyms. Give it to a friend to try to read. You might also want to attempt making your own abbreviations for terms.

Vocabulary

Jargon/Technical Language

Jargon is usually very localized language, known only to a select group. It can sound like nonsense to the untrained ear. Industry and business, however, use jargon that is particular to the job. Computer jargon, for example, would include terms such as **reboot, hard drive, modem, Internet, RAM**. These are **technical terms**, or jargon, particular to the area.

> **Jargon** is used often, but is usually understood only by the group or industry using it. Use jargon sparingly in your writing, especially if it is of such a specialized type that few would understand it.

1. Underline terms in this list that you think are **jargon** terms for the computer industry.

   boot sector virus   trucking   laser printer   nebula   microprocessor   flooring monitor   hardware   initiate launch sequence   read only memory   cache   zip drive

2. Write some **jargon** terms that are used at your school. Remember, these would be terms understood by all to be school terms, such as **assembly** and **announcements**.

   _____

   _____

   _____

3. Think of an area that you are familiar with. Write some **jargon** terms used in that area. For example, think of jargon used in the music industry: **CD**, **videos**, and so on.

   _____

   _____

   _____

4. We hear **jargon** used all of the time in sports broadcasts. Write a short paragraph that uses sports jargon for a particular sport. You may want to write it as if you were a sportscaster.

   _____

   _____

   _____

   _____

   _____

   _____

   _____

   _____

   _____

 Find examples of jargon in materials such as magazines, newspapers, and books. Listen for jargon on the TV. With a partner, create a list of "jargonese."

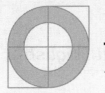

Vocabulary

Formal and Informal English 1

Formal English is the acceptable language of an English-speaking country.

Informal English is colloquial or casual everyday language. Formal English is that which is taught in schools. Informal English is made up of terms and idioms found in common speech, such as slang, jargon, and so on. Look at these examples.

Formal English should be used when we write essays and other such types of informational work. It should also be used in most story writing. However, **informal English** can be used in dialogue in stories to add a more "real" feel to the writing.

Formal: The skater hit the crossbar.

Informal: Yeah, the guy skating slammed into the crossbar, right?

1. Indicate whether each sentence is **formal** or **informal**.

   (a) You got me, I can't tell if he's coming or going! _____

   (b) The light shone with a glistening effect on the trees. _____

   (c) We started the journey with our hopes high and our spirits buoyed. _____

   (d) Ya hits the ball, Willie, ya hits the ball. _____

   (e) Jeremy's a creep, if you ask me. _____

2. **Informal English** is often very conversational: you can picture people talking in a casual, less than formal way. Rewrite this conversation in informal English. Use slang and jargon where necessary, but keep the main idea of the original.

   "I had a dream last night," said Cristina.

   "What was it about?" questioned Liz.

   "In it, I saw a wonderful place, where beautiful buildings lined long, winding streets," Cristina sighed. "It was wonderful!"

   "I will say that it was! You certainly had a wonderful dream!" replied Liz.

   "Yes! Just think about all of the wonderful things I could do in a place like that!" said Cristina.

   _____

   _____

   _____

   _____

   _____

   _____

   _____

   _____

Now, go to the next page for more practice with **formal** and **informal** English.

Vocabulary

Formal and Informal English 2

On this page, write a sample piece in **formal English**, and then one in **informal English**. You may select a writing that exists and write it in the opposite style (formal or informal), or you may write an original piece. Good luck!

Think: changing a formal advertisement copy into an informal one; taking a section of a textbook and writing it informally; writing a typical telephone conversation in formal English; and so on.

Formal English Writing

_____

_____

_____

_____

_____

_____

_____

_____

_____

_____

Informal English Writing

_____

_____

_____

_____

_____

_____

_____

_____

_____

_____

_____

_____

 Try an experiment. Use formal English in an informal setting (such as a conversation in the cafeteria). Observe how the use of this form of English causes reactions among your friends.

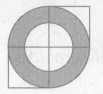

Vocabulary

English has an abundance of words from many languages. Look at these examples.

ketchup: from the Malay *kechap* for **fish sauce**
algebra: from the Arabic *al-jabr* for the **science of reuniting**

We use these borrowed words as if they were part of English all along!

1. Here are some short lists of **borrowed words** and their **origins**.

   Spanish: amigo, bonanza, canyon, corral, chili, macho, patio, plaza, stampede, tomato
   Scandinavian: egg, ill, saga, ski, skin, skirt, smorgasbord
   French: beret, bistro, cadet, chef, collage, critique, lecture, nonchalant, rapport, revue, suite, toupee
   Italian: balcony, balloon, bravo, fiasco, pilot, regatta, replica, studio, trombone, violin

   Write three sentences using borrowed words from the lists. For example:

   My amigo and I travelled through the canyon in our hot-air balloon with a seasoned pilot.

   (a) _____

   _____

   (b) _____

   _____

   (c) _____

   _____

2. English also uses borrowed expressions. Look at these examples.

   à la carte: from the French for **according to (from) the menu**
   c'est la vie: from the French for **that's life**

   Use these **borrowed expressions** in sentences to show their meanings. Use a dictionary to check the meanings of the phrases.

   chutzpah   raison d'être   per annum   déjà vu

   (a) _____

   _____

   (b) _____

   _____

   (c) _____

   _____

   (d) _____

   _____

Find examples of borrowed words and phrases in your daily readings. Use some of the newer ones in your writings.

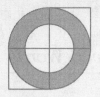

Vocabulary

Etymology

Etymology is the study of the origin of words. Discover some interesting word origins on this page.

> **Etymology** comes from the Greek *etumologia* for **true sense of the word** (*etumon*) and **the study of** (*ologia*).

1. Use the **word origin** clues to guess what these words are.

   (a) This word comes from the Greek *oikonomia* for "managing a household." Today, we use it to mean the money system or management of resources. _____

   (b) This word, often used to mean **a group of criminals**, comes from the Old Norse *gangr* meaning **group** or **journey**. _____

   (c) This brief interval of time comes from the Latin *momentum*: **to move**. _____

   (d) This **walking with difficulty** word comes from the Middle English *hobblen*. _____

   (e) This word meaning **to shake with or as if cold** comes from the Middle English *chiveren*. _____

   (f) This word that describes large sections of grass comes from the Old English *lunde*. _____

2. Describe the **origins** of these words, as best you can. You may want to ask others for help or look up information from other sources.

   (a) Your first name: _____

   _____

   _____

   (b) The name of your city, town, village, etc.: _____

   _____

   _____

   (c) The name of your school: _____

   _____

   _____

   _____

   (d) A word or term you use often: _____

   _____

   _____

   _____

 Investigate the origin of the name of one of your favourite singers or musical bands. Report your finding to some friends.

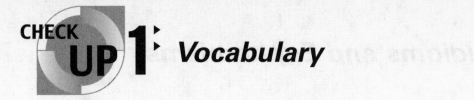

1. Underline the **prefixes** and **suffixes** in these words.

   monorail   kingdom   overact   subway   friendship   childish   toward   hyperactive

2. Make proper words with these **prefixes** and **suffixes**. Make at least five words in all.

   dis-: _____

   mid-: _____

   out-: _____

   -ate: _____

   -ness: _____

3. Give **antonyms** for these words.

   night: _____ toward: _____

   unclean: _____ allow: _____

   maximum: _____ guilty: _____

   Use at least one antonym pair in a sentence.

   _____

   _____

4. Give at least one **synonym** for each of these words.

   house: _____ leader: _____

   courage: _____ run: _____

   Use at least one **pair of synonyms** in a sentence.

   _____

   _____

5. Use each **homonym** pair in a sentence.

   their, there: _____

   desert, dessert: _____

   guessed, guest: _____

   paws, pause: _____

6. Write a sentence for each **homonym** trio.

   to, too, two: _____

   _____

   right, rite, write: _____

   _____

CHECK UP 2 ▸ *Idioms and Euphemisms*

1. What is an **idiom**? _____

   _____

2. Write what these **idioms** mean.

   (a) learn word for word: _____

   (b) take up arms: _____

   (c) get the better of: _____

   (d) full of hot air: _____

   (e) walking papers: _____

3. Use two of the **idioms** in Activity #2 in sentences that show their meanings.

   (a) _____

   _____

   (b) _____

   _____

4. What is a **euphemism**? _____

   _____

5. Write a **euphemistic term** for each of these.

   (a) deaf: _____

   (b) sick: _____

   (c) Shut your mouth! _____

   (d) short: _____

   (e) dead: _____

6. Use three of the **euphemisms** in Activity #5 in sentences that show their meanings.

   (a) _____

   _____

   (b) _____

   _____

   (c) _____

   _____

CHECK UP 3 ▸ Clichés and Proverbs

1. What is a **cliché**? _____

   _____

2. Write what each of these **clichés** mean.

   (a) at death's door: _____

   (b) beat about the bush: _____

   (c) raining cats and dogs: _____

3. Use two of the **clichés** in Activity #2 in sentences that show their meanings.

   (a) _____

   _____

   (b) _____

   _____

4. What is a **proverb**, in the context of writing? _____

   _____

5. Write what each of these **proverbs** means.

   (a) A rolling stone gathers no moss. _____

   _____

   (b) One person's garbage is another person's treasure. _____

   (c) Every cloud has a silver lining. _____

   _____

   (d) What goes around, comes around. _____

6. Use two of the **proverbs** in Activity #5 in sentences that show their meanings.

   (a) _____

   _____

   (b) _____

   _____

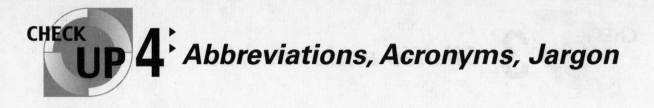
1. (a) What is an **abbreviation**? _____

    _____

    (b) Write the **long forms** for these **abbreviations**.

    Cdn. _____   Ave. _____

    U.S. _____   pkg. _____

    Sat. _____   TV _____

    (c) Write **abbreviations** for these words.

    January _____   Wednesday _____

    revolutions per minute _____   as soon as possible _____

2. Write a sentence that uses at least one **abbreviation**.

    _____

3. (a) What is an **acronym**? _____

    _____

    (b) Write an **acronym** you know and give its **longer form**.

    _____ : _____

4. Use an **acronym** in a sentence to show its meaning.

    _____

5. (a) What is **jargon**? _____

    _____

    (b) Give at least three examples of **computer jargon**. _____

    _____

    (c) Give at least three examples of **jargon** you know. Identify what area the jargon is for
    (e.g., skateboarding jargon).

    _____

    _____

6. Write two sentences that use **jargon**. They can be linked together or two different
    sentences.

    (a) _____

    _____

    (b) _____

    _____

1. What is the difference between **formal** and **informal** English? _____

    _____

    _____

2. For each situation, indicate whether it needs **formal** or **informal** English.

    (a) writing an essay: _____

    (b) telling a joke: _____

    (c) talking to a friend on the telephone: _____

    (d) ordering a pizza on the telephone: _____

    (e) giving a speech in the auditorium: _____

    (f) completing a history assignment: _____

    (g) talking to friends at the bus stop: _____

    (h) explaining your absence from school to the vice-principal: _____

    (i) asking a friend out on a date: _____

    (j) giving directions to a tourist: _____

3. Write a short paragraph (including dialogue, if needed) on the following situation in **formal** English. After you have done this, rewrite your paragraph in **informal** English.

    Reporting to the Attendance Office after you missed your bus

    Formal:

    _____

    _____

    _____

    _____

    _____

    _____

    Informal:

    _____

    _____

    _____

    _____

    _____

    _____

    _____

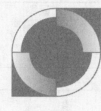

Unit 3

Spelling, Capitalization, Punctuation

1. Break these words into **syllables**. Put an accent on the **stressed syllable**.

    precede: _____   gymnasium: _____

    adolescents: _____   necessary: _____

    commercial: _____   sufficient: _____

    technical: _____   international: _____

2. Make these words **plural**. Change the spelling accordingly.

    wolf: _____   mouse: _____

    oasis: _____   child: _____

    cactus: _____   curriculum: _____

3. Read these sentences. Underline any word that seems **misspelled**. Rewrite the sentences with corrected spellings.

    (a) The tain wound slowly throgh the mountane pass before exitting near the vilage.

    _____

    _____

    (b) Everybody sat patienly watcvhing the game, when the buzer sounded, ending this disaster.

    _____

    _____

    (c) "There arent enough parts to go around!" yeled the direcer at the expectent cast.

    _____

    _____

    (d) When they arived at the waters edge, they saw what the Admiral had been talking about: vast amount of seeweed, mysteriosly washed up on shor.

    _____

    _____

    (e) The concert was going well, when all of a sudden, Rami jumped up on stage and started danceing with the band.

    _____

    _____

4. Make a list of ten words that you find difficult to spell. Check the **spelling** of each word in a dictionary. Compare your list with a partner.

    _____   _____

    _____   _____

    _____   _____

FOCUS ON: Capitalization

1. Indicate at least three instances when **capital letters** should be used.

   _____

   _____

   _____

2. Read these sentences. Circle letters that should be capitalized. Rewrite the sentences with corrected **capital letters**.

   (a) i should have crossed delaney drive, but went to holdstom court instead.

   _____

   (b) We had fun at the action arcade last night, just before we saw the movie at watson's cineplay theatre.

   _____

   _____

   (c) However you come up with the answer, todd, do tell us how tanjah was able to calculate the distance to jupiter.

   _____

   _____

   (d) A very disgruntled shopper at the abstract art shoppe complained about the presence of too many group of seven paintings.

   _____

   _____

   (e) "Where are we going?" asked Jerold, always wanting to know which way the oldsmobile was pointed.

   _____

   _____

3. Use **capital letters** correctly when completing these.

   (a) the address of your school: _____

   _____

   (b) the titles of your favourite movies (list three or four): _____

   _____

   _____

   (c) song titles from a favourite group or singer (list at least two): _____

   _____

   (d) a book you have read recently: _____

   (e) a country you would like to visit: _____

   (f) a TV program not worth watching (in your opinion): _____

   (g) a TV program that you would recommend: _____

FOCUS ON: Punctuation

1. Identify these **punctuation marks**.

… _____   " " _____   ; _____

: _____   ! _____   ( ) _____

' _____   , _____   [ ] _____

- _____   — _____   . _____

2. Rewrite these sentences using the correct **punctuation marks**.

(a) We have to get going right now yelled Jason standing by the side of the car

_____

(b) I wonder what happens next is it possible she never read my message

_____

(c) The movie was just so so and I do mean that but the popcorn wasnt bad

_____

(d) Yesterday I hired twenty new managers to help with the company declared the CEO

_____

(e) Look at this list five shirts ten pairs of pants two bags and a hat Whoever came up with this stuff

_____

3. Write a short paragraph (or a series of separate sentences) using all of the types of **punctuation** in Activity #1.

_____

_____

_____

_____

_____

_____

_____

_____

_____

_____

_____

_____

_____

_____

Spelling

Use these **spelling tips** when you are writing.

- Use *i* before *e* except after *c*, or when it sounds like *a* as in **weigh**: receipt, field, neighbour
- Drop the final silent *e* when adding a **suffix** beginning with a **vowel**: tame: taming
- Keep the final silent *e* when adding a **suffix** beginning with a **consonant**: blame: blameless
- Change *y* to *i* when *y* is preceded by a **consonant**: try: tried
- Do not change *y* to *i* when *y* is preceded by a **vowel** or when adding *ing*: pay: pays; try: trying
- Double the final consonant when the **final consonant** is preceded by a **single vowel**: hop: hopping
- Do not double the final consonant when the **final consonant** is preceded by **two vowels**: repair: repairing
- Do not double the final consonant when **two or more consonants** at the word's end are preceded by a **single vowel**: jump: jumping
- Add *s* for plurals of most nouns: boy: boys; patio: patios
- Add *es* when the plural is pronounced as another **syllable**: church: churches
- Add *es* when the noun ending in *o* is preceded by a **consonant**: tomato: tomatoes
- Change *f* or *fe* to *v* then add *es*: wolf: wolves

1. Use the **spelling tips** to correct these misspelled words.

    stoping: _____   beleive: _____

    blamming: _____   radioes: _____

    defyed: _____   despairring: _____

    calfes: _____   wiegh: _____

2. Another spelling tip is: **Read your work backward, word for word, checking for misspelled words.** Read these sentences backward, word for word. Circle any words you think are misspelled. Check these words in a dictionary. Rewrite the corrected sentences.

    (a) The van sped around the cornerr careening into the sinpost, hiting two cars befour stopping at the ege of Blaker Strret.

    _____

    _____

    (b) Polic surounded the vehacle, demandding that the driveer get out of the van.

    _____

    _____

 Use the spelling tips on this page when you proofread your own writing, checking for spelling errors.

Use the **spelling tips** from the previous page to help as you proofread (check over) the spelling on this page.

1. Read this paragraph. **Proofread** it for spelling errors. Circle misspelled words. Check the words you have indicated in a dictionary. Rewrite the paragraph with the correctly spelled words.

   It wqas a terribl thing to wach: rivers of mud flowwing throuh the twon, prople runing to get out of the way, whole building smashed and destoied. We looked at the TV screan in awe at the power of this menase. What could we do? we thout. We were in another part of the world, and we felt so helppless. At that moment, a person came on the screan, describing how everyone could lend a hand by calling a toll-free number. She said we could donat clothing and food to the Relief Fund. That was it! We caled rite then. Hopfully, we might help to make a diference.

   _____

   _____

   _____

   _____

   _____

   _____

2. Write a paragraph about an issue that has been in the news recently. **Proofread** your paragraph using the spelling tips. Check any words you think are misspelled in a dictionary. Rewrite the words with the correct spelling down the sides of the page.

   _____

   _____

   _____

   _____

   _____

   _____

   _____

   _____

   _____

   _____

Proofread a newspaper article. Make a list of the misspelled words. Check a dictionary for the correct spellings.

Spelling

Use capital letters

- at the **beginning** of sentences: The train stops here.

- for the pronoun **I**: When will **I** get a chance?

- for **proper nouns**: **D**eena, **W**innipeg, **T**oyota

- for the first, last, and all major words in the **titles** of books, movies, and so on:
  The **N**ature of **T**hings; **A**nne of **G**reen **G**ables; **G**one with the **W**ind

- for the **titles** of persons when the title is used as part of the proper name:
  Reverend Mika Prestley

> Be sure with **capital letters**: check in a dictionary if you are not sure. Some words are capitalized when you think they shouldn't be.

1. Read these sentences, checking for **capital letter** usage. Rewrite the sentences with correct capital letter usage.

   (a) the planet jupiter may be the largest in the solar system, but it is mostly huge layers of deadly gas.

   _____

   _____

   (b) humans continue to search space for inhabitable planets, including mars, one of the closest neighbours to earth.

   _____

   _____

   (c) launches from cape canaveral in florida are spectacular as the nasa rockets speed upward into the outer atmosphere.

   _____

   _____

   (d) one day, we may celebrate birthdays on the moon, or on one of the larger moons of jupiter such as ganymede or io.

   _____

   _____

2. Write sentences on the following topics. Name the items indicated. Use **capital letters** correctly.

   (a) your favourite singing group:_____

   _____

   (b) a street near where you live: _____

   _____

   (c) a mall you shop at: _____

   _____

   (d) your school: _____

   _____

▶▶ ***Check for creative uses of capital letters in places such as song titles and group names.***

This page and the next will help you practise **comma usage**.

In these sentences, **commas** are used correctly.

(a) We brought hammers, saws, nails, and lunches to the site.

(b) Jamie was happy with the party, and Wayne stole the show!

(c) Kyle, who had to read the entire chapter, spoke clearly to the class.

(d) Wilfrid Laurier, a Canadian Prime Minister, led the country in the early 1900s.

(e) When we entered the fairgrounds, we saw what everyone was talking about.

(f) For the truly adventurous traveller, the Amazon is the place to go.

(g) Strange, delightful creatures await you there.

(h) Every city (e.g., Toronto) has a city hall.

(i) Charlene, do you know where our city hall is?

(j) January 1, 2000, is a date that will cause computer buffs to think back.

1. Read these sentences for **comma usage**. Rewrite sentences that need comma usage corrections.

    (a) We, filed into the train, the Via train from Montreal, to Toronto.

    _____

    (b) For everyone on the bus the trip was well worth the price.

    _____

    (c) Bill Gates the computer entrepreneur became the youngest billionaire during the 1990s.

    _____

    (d) When we called his name Giles turned around.

    _____

    (e) Abigail, do you know how to drive a bus?

    _____

2. Write two sentences that use **commas** correctly.

    (a) _____

    _____

    (b) _____

    _____

 Read through advertisements, checking for comma usage. Why might advertisers be creative with their uses of commas?

3. Check this rough copy of a report for **comma usage**. Rewrite the report with corrected comma usage.

The time spent, on building the Greig Office Tower, at Main and Adelaide, has moved into that realm of "too, much." As financiers responsible for shareholders, money, we question the ability of the Adler Construction, Co. to complete the job before the next, fiscal year.

With time, money work orders all being held up because of poor, planning, we are forced to submit our proposal, for relinquishing the Adler Co. of all, further work to be done on this project, and wish to negotiate a new contract, with the Solid Mark Builders of Alberta, to complete this project.

_____

_____

_____

_____

_____

_____

_____

_____

_____

4. Add **commas** where necessary to this advertisement copy.

> **No one not even Barky himself could have been prepared**
>
> **for the taste the smell or the greatness of**
>
> *Bone Bits Puppy Rations*
>
> **the new dog food from Animal Smarts!**
>
> **Dogs will eat and eat this new chow! They'll run jump leap even crawl out of bed for its delectable mouth-watering taste!**
>
> **For the discerning pet we have created this treat.**
>
> **Buy it now buy it tomorrow but BUY it before Barky finds out you didn't!**

5. Write a short advertisement for a product of your choice. Use **commas** properly in your copy.

_____

_____

_____

 ▶ *Check how commas are used in song lyrics. Make a list of lyrics that use commas "creatively."*

Punctuation *Colons and Semicolons*

In these sentences, **colons** and **semicolons** are used correctly.

(a) The players need these: skates, sticks, pads, and proper gloves.

(b) Players work very hard at practice; they need to get ready for each game.

(c) Blaine always told us this: "Don't forget the past; it will come back to haunt you."

(d) We arrived at 9:15; we left at 11:45.

(e) Sara read from Matthew 4:2–4; Jason quoted from Sotah 3:16a.

(f) The plane touched down in London, England; Paris, France; and Brussels, Belgium.

1. Rewrite these sentences adding **colons** and **semicolons** where necessary.

   (a) Our bus left at 355 we arrived at the game an hour later.

   _____

   _____

   (b) Always remember to carry the following your books, your pencils, your sketchpads, and your imaginations.

   _____

   _____

   (c) Shirley was famous for telling us "You can't always have fun at the expense of others."

   _____

   _____

   (d) They came from Vancouver, British Columbia Edmonton, Alberta Moose Jaw, Saskatchewan and Halifax, Nova Scotia.

   _____

   _____

2. Write five sentences that use **colons** and **semicolons**. You could put your sentences together in a paragraph if you wish.

   _____

   _____

   _____

   _____

   _____

   _____

 Check print materials for uses of colons and semicolons. Practise with these and other uses of these punctuation marks in your writings.

In these sentences, **quotation marks** are used correctly.

(a) "I found my way to the concert!" yelled Sharron.

(b) We read "The Monkey's Paw" by Saki yesterday.

(c) Try not to call Jeremy by his nickname, "Blinkey."

Quotations within **quotation marks** use **single quotation marks**.

"We remember reading 'The Monkey's Paw' long ago," said Marie.

1. Rewrite these sentences inserting **quotation marks** where necessary.

    (a) I always had a good time at Charlie's parties, sighed Ramone.

    _____

    _____

    (b) The story We Are Winners By Choice by Mildred Owens is a must-read on the subject list.

    _____

    _____

    (c) The train stops here said the ticket master. You had better get your bags ready.

    _____

    _____

    (d) They were always using the term slagmen whenever the other team stepped onto the field.

    _____

    _____

    (e) Just then, Mark called out I want everyone's attention! We have made it into the finals!

    _____

    _____

    (f) I just heard The Way To Nunavut by Inuk Men, and it was great! said Melanie.

    _____

    _____

    (g) He was known for saying We must get on with it! replied Treena.

    _____

    _____

2. Write a sentence of your own that has at least two usages of **quotation marks**.

    _____

    _____

 Find examples of creative quotation mark usage in materials you read. Use some of the ideas you find in your own writing.

Punctuation

In these sentences, **quotation punctuation** is used correctly.

(a) "I wanted the vegetarian platter," said Jeananne.

(b) "We are all out of that dish," replied the waiter, "but we do have plenty of green salads."

(c) Jeananne retorted, "Is that what I came here for?"

(d) She actually said "Is that what I came here for!"

In dialogue with quotations, begin a **new paragraph** for each new speaker.

"We had so much fun," said Roland. "It was what I always wanted to do."

"Yes," said Lee, "we hadn't done this with our families before. It was great!"

Roland replied, "I think that this should be the start of a long tradition."

"Absolutely!"

Write a conversation between two or more characters. Use **quotation marks** and **quotation punctuation** based on the tips given above and on the previous page. Use a variety of approaches with the quotations.

_____

_____

_____

_____

_____

_____

_____

_____

_____

_____

_____

_____

_____

_____

_____

 Proofread newspaper stories for incorrect use of quote punctuation. Cut the articles out and keep them for future discussion with classmates.

Punctuation

Dashes, Parentheses,
Brackets, Diagonals

In these sentences, **dashes**, **parentheses**, **brackets**, and **diagonals** have been used correctly.

(a) We might take the train—actually, we'll take my car.

(b) The trip—one of the best ever—will remain in our memories.

(c) Fun times, great food—it was a partier's dream!

(d) The essay (due on Thursday) was on everyone's mind Wednesday night.

(e) The essays (what a lot of writing) were handed in on time.

(f) Try these for practice: (1) stretch your arms, (2) grasp the bat, and (3) swing wildly.

(g) "Now, when we see them [junior students], don't panic!" said the Student Council President.

(h) This will give you a pass/fail grade mark.

(i) "The lines of trees stood / Beyond the valley walls, / And I couldn't stop but wonder: / What lay beyond the malls."

> **Diagonals** are often used to separate lines of poetry or song lyrics when they're printed out of context from their original source.

1. Rewrite these sentences adding **dashes**, **parentheses**, **brackets**, and **diagonals** where necessary.

(a) The delivery due at 3:00 p.m. was late as usual.

_____

(b) If you run this course, you will receive an accept reject notice from the coach.

_____

(c) Make sure that you complete these: 1 the laundry, 2 the shopping, and 3 the party list.

_____

(d) This game the best we ever played will be remembered for years!

_____

2. Write two sentences for each of these punctuation forms: **dashes**, **parentheses**, **brackets**, and **diagonals**.

(a) _____

(b) _____

(a) _____

(b) _____

(a) _____

(b) _____

(a) _____

(b) _____

▶▶ *Find examples of these punctuation marks in printed material. Observe how others use them.*

Spelling, Capitalization, Punctuation

Read this selection. Check it for errors in **spelling**, **capitalization**, and **punctuation**. Rewrite the paragraph with corrections in these three areas.

> Always read through a selection a few times each time checking for something different: **spelling**, then **capitalization**, then **punctuation**. This will help you to catch all of the errors.

i wonderd how it had, happened Two days ago; my friends and I had left for a coampeng trip in Algonquin park. and thougt it was going to be the best vacation ever First there was and I thingk Im rite on this the blown tire on the highway? Jeremy had to fix it as he was the only won with the know how in changeing tires next came the storm and I do mean storm, We barely got the tent set up using a new tool, the gripper tightener to steady it when the storm hit us with 1 a gale force, 2 wet pounding rain, and 3 lightning everywhere: Soon, everythin was wet food, clothing tools fishing gear even our book

How about givbing me a hand yelled jeremy as he tried to steady the canvas I need to get everything the supplies steadied in this wind

We scambled over to him just in time to see the tent go off into the trees. we spent the rest of the night gathering up our gear then sleeping in the car; What a begining to a vacashun—

_____

_____

_____

_____

_____

_____

_____

_____

_____

_____

_____

_____

_____

_____

_____

_____

Spelling, Capitalization, Punctuation

Use this page to practise with correct **spelling**, **capitalization**, and **punctuation** in your own writing. Select one of the following writing ideas:

- an advertisement for a new product;

- a story on a topic of your choice;

- a review of a group's new CD in a magazine;

- a newspaper story reporting a breaking news story;

- a poem on a topic of your choice;

- a set of directions, such as a recipe.

> You may want to use this page in the following way:
> - write the entire piece on this page as a rough;
> - use half of the page for the rough, half for the good copy;
> - use a clean sheet of paper for the good copy.

Write your assignment and check for correct **spelling** and **capitalization**. Use at least six forms of **punctuation**, including quotation marks, in your writing.

_____

_____

_____

_____

_____

_____

_____

_____

_____

_____

_____

_____

_____

_____

_____

_____

_____

_____

_____

_____

_____

_____

 Check a song lyric on a CD insert, or an article you have read that seems to have imaginative or incorrect usages of spelling, capitalization, and punctuation. Indicate where you think the errors are, then discuss your ideas for corrections with a partner or small group.

1. Write four **spelling tips** that are used to remind writers about correct spelling.

   (a) _____

   _____

   (b) _____

   _____

   (c) _____

   _____

   (d) _____

   _____

2. Write two **spelling tips** of your own that help you to spell words correctly.

   (a) _____

   _____

   (b) _____

   _____

3. Give three **proofreading tips** that help as you check your writing for spelling errors.

   (a) _____

   _____

   (b) _____

   _____

   (c) _____

   _____

4. One tip to help in spelling words correctly is to know their **syllables**. Divide each of these words into syllables. Underline the **accented** (stressed) **syllable**. (HINT: Say the word first, breaking it into its syllables. Place the stress on different syllables to get the one that sounds right.)

   temporary: _____   quotation: _____

   incomplete: _____   reference: _____

   geography: _____   society: _____

   spelling: _____   follower: _____

   gargantuan: _____   technology: _____

   compound: _____   cucumber: _____

   independent: _____   auditorium: _____

   encyclopedia: _____   bibliography: _____

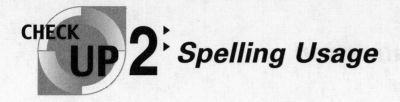

CHECK UP 2 ▸ Spelling Usage

1. Match the words below with their **meanings**. Use a dictionary to help you, if needed.

   irritate cynic orientation maximum landlocked blatant obstinate

   (a) _____ the act of locating or positioning.

   (b) _____ loud and noisy in an unpleasant way.

   (c) _____ to bother, often incessantly.

   (d) _____ completely surrounded by land.

   (e) _____ the ultimate or greatest.

   (f) _____ one who believes all people are motivated by selfishness.

   (g) _____ adhering to an opinion or attitude in a stubborn way.

2. Write a sentence for each of the words above, having each word show its **meaning** from context. Use the meaning clues to help you. Check the **spelling** of all of your sentence words.

   (a) _____

   _____

   (b) _____

   _____

   (c) _____

   _____

   (d) _____

   _____

   (e) _____

   _____

   (f) _____

   _____

   (g) _____

   _____

3. Write a short selection on a topic of your choice. Read over what you have written, checking for words that you may have misspelled. Circle these words. Try to correct them using **spelling tips**, then check your corrected words with a dictionary.

   _____

   _____

   _____

   _____

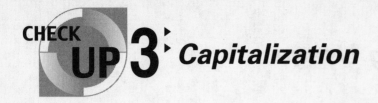

CHECK UP 3 · *Capitalization*

1. Give three examples of the use of **capital letters** in writing.

   (a) _____

   (b) _____

   (c) _____

2. Check these sentences for **capitalization**. Rewrite the sentences with corrected use of capital letters.

   (a) the gift shop in the fieldcrest mall sold out of all copies of *the dangerous life* by milton shenweld on Tuesday.

   _____

   _____

   (b) Send it to 358 centre street, fredericton, new brunswick by friday march 24.

   _____

   _____

   (c) we had to finish watching "the only singer from wiarton" on the showbiz network before we could finally leave commander auditorium.

   _____

   (d) I've read *too many players on the team* by cindy matton, but i never thought they would make a hollywood movie out of such a trite piece of obvious fiction!

   _____

   _____

   (e) whenever geena sees us walking toward her down sheridan hall, she ducks into room 132, the english classroom.

   _____

   _____

3. Write three sentences on topics of your choice (you could put them together in a paragraph). Use at least two types of **capitalization** in each sentence.

   _____

   _____

   _____

   _____

   _____

   _____

CHECK UP 4 ▸ Punctuation 1

1. Give ten **punctuation marks** and the use for each.

    (a) _____ : _____

    (b) _____ : _____

    (c) _____ : _____

    (d) _____ : _____

    (e) _____ : _____

    (f) _____ : _____

    (g) _____ : _____

    (h) _____ : _____

    (i) _____ : _____

    (j) _____ : _____

2. Punctuate these sentences correctly with **end punctuation**.

    (a) Where have all the students gone____

    (b) We felt that the best way to get this done was by calling everyone together____

    (c) I can't believe I won first prize____

    (d) When you get there, will you call us____

    (e) Get the ball____

3. Add **punctuation** where necessary in these sentences. Rewrite the sentences with the correct punctuation.

    (a) The players needed pads shoes helmets face guards and a winning spirit.

    _____

    (b) It was all we could do the rest is up to them now.

    _____

    (c) Here's what you need to get this job done a lot of determination and a little madness

    _____

    (d) Buddy Holly an influential rock and roll singer died in 1959.

    _____

    (e) You have the correct change don't you

    _____

    (f) Wild crazy screams came from the bungee jumpers.

    _____

    (g) I cant do this because I wouldnt study when the teacher suggested I shouldve.

    _____

CHECK UP 4 : *Punctuation 2*

1. Add **punctuation** where necessary in these sentences. Rewrite the sentences with the correct punctuation.

    (a) We might go to the movies on second thought lets watch a video at home.

    _____

    (b) That concert one I regret missing was the musical event of the year.

    _____

    (c) Your grade on this paper will be a pass fail.

    _____

    (d) "We saw fifteen of them mallard ducks swimming up stream," said the naturalist.

    _____

    (e) Its her twenty first birthday and already shes self employed.

    _____

    (f) The essay due this Thursday was handed in late by everyone.

    _____

2. Write a short selection on a topic of your choice. Use at least eight types of **punctuation** correctly in context in your writing.

    _____
    _____
    _____
    _____
    _____
    _____
    _____
    _____
    _____
    _____
    _____
    _____
    _____
    _____
    _____
    _____
    _____

1. Indicate when **quotation marks** are used.

   _____

   _____

2. How is a **quotation** shown within a **quotation**? Write a sentence showing this.

   _____

   _____

3. Punctuate these sentences correctly with **quotation marks** and internal **quotation punctuation**. Rewrite the sentences on the lines.

   (a) I think I know the answer yelled Fishburne I just figured it out.

   _____

   (b) The officer called Get out of the way as a galloping horse ran by.

   _____

   (c) When Greel said To be or not to be... what did he mean questioned Kali.

   _____

   (d) The dogs will find the trail said Morton even if it takes them all day.

   _____

   (e) We noticed your car replied Shirley That was how we knew you were here.

   _____

4. Write a short dialogue between two people. Use **quotation marks** and **quotation punctuation** correctly.

   _____

   _____

   _____

   _____

   _____

   _____

   _____

   _____

   _____

Unit 4

Grammar and Usage

FOCUS ON: Grammar

1. What is the difference between a **common noun** and a **proper noun**? _Common_ _nouns are not specific, and proper nouns are specific and are_ _capitalized._

2. What is an **antecedent** when referring to **nouns** and **pronouns**? _____
_____

3. Rewrite these sentences using **pronouns** for the **nouns** in boldface.
   (a) **Joanne** read the **book**. _She read it._
   (b) **Marie** and **Zoe** took the **train**. _They took it._
   (c) Many **students** attended the **game**. _They attended it._

4. (a) Write a sentence with a **verb** in the **active voice**.
   I am writin a story.
   _____

   (b) Write a sentence with a **verb** in the **passive voice**.
   The story was written.
   _____

5. For each verb in the **present tense**, give its **past** and **future tense**.

	Past Tense	**Future Tense**
believe	believed	will believe
sing	sang	will sing
write	wrote	will write
began	began	will begin
decide	decided	will decide
hear	heard	will hear
meander	meandered	will meander
concede	conceded	will concede

6. Circle the **verb** that shows **correct usage** in each sentence.

   (a) The team (practise, (practises)) every day after classes.

   (b) Our coach (helps, (helped)) us win the championship last year.

   (c) Whenever we (gets, (get)) down after a loss, she (make, (makes)) us ((believe), believes) in ourselves.

   (d) During the games, we remain (focus, (focussed)) as a team as we ((play), plays) our best.

   (e) Each time we ((practise), practises), we ((get), gets) a little closer to our goal.

FOCUS ON: Sentences

1. Write **sentences** of the following types.

   interrogative: _____

   declarative: _____

   exclamatory: _____

   imperative: _____

2. Put a diagonal between the **subject** and **predicate** in each of these sentences.

   (a) The long, tiring journey ended outside of the old inn.

   (b) Many people stormed the doors of the bank.

   (c) We tried to call you at noon!

   (d) A very temperamental young actor threw an embarrassing tantrum on the movie set.

   (e) Too few of the graduates took advantage of the scholarships to the college.

3. For each **main clause**, write a **subordinate clause**.

   (a) The day seemed to last forever _____

   (b) _____, we found our way home.

   (c) The final buzzer sounded _____

   (d) A second opinion was spoken _____

   (e) _____, I knew it was over.

4. Combine each pair of **simple sentences** into a **compound sentence**.

   (a) Jennifer liked to swim. She enjoyed her job as a lifeguard.

   _____

   (b) A rabid fox jumped over the log. We dove for cover.

   _____

5. Here is an example of a **complex** sentence: **After we won the race, we celebrated long into the night.** Write three complex sentences on topics of your choice. Use the sample sentence as a guide to form.

   (a) _____

   _____

   (b) _____

   _____

   (c) _____

   _____

Parts of Speech

A **noun** is a word that names a person, place, thing, or idea. Nouns can be

- **concrete:** elephant, violin, car, airplane, tree, chocolate

- **abstract:** love, faith, friendliness, separation

- **proper:** Toronto, William Bond, Canada, Arctic Ocean

- **common:** woman, city, mountain, lake

- **compound:** strawberry, sister-in-law, well-wisher, home run, Rolling Stones

- **singular:** whale, child, woman, deer

- **plural:** whales, children, women, deer

- **collective:** herd, pair, team, squad

- **possessive:** Jeanette's, committee's, Montréal's

> Remember these tips:
> - **concrete:** names something physical that can be perceived by one or more of the senses;
> - **abstract:** names something that cannot be perceived by the senses;
> - **proper:** names a particular person, place, or thing and starts with a capital letter;
> - **common:** names a person, place, or thing in a non-specific way and does not start with a capital letter;
> - **compound:** has more that one word and is written as one word, with a hyphen, or as two separate words;
> - **singular:** means "one";
> - **plural:** means "more than one";
> - **collective:** names a group of individuals (plural) but is singular in form
> - **possessive:** shows ownership or belonging with the use of the apostrophe.

1. Underline the **nouns** in each sentence. Using the above list, indicate what **types** they are.

   (a) The <u>vessel</u> entered the <u>harbour</u> by the solid <u>moonlight</u> shining on the still <u>waters</u>.

   Vessel - Concrete, harbour - Concrete, moonlight - Compound, Waters - Plural

   (b) Every <u>woman</u> and <u>child</u> ran for <u>cover</u> from the <u>volcano's fury</u>.

   _____

   (c) His <u>daughter-in-law</u> visited after stopping at the mall's department store.

   daughter-in-law - Compound , _____

2. Write two sentences using **possessive nouns** in each.

   (a) _____

   _____

   (b) _____

   _____

3. Give the **plurals** of these singular nouns. Check your plurals in a dictionary if necessary.

   man: *Men*   chief: *Chiefes*

   wolf: *Wolves*   avenue: *avenues*

   history: *histories*   tax: *taxes*

   shelf: *Shelves*   journey: ~~journees~~ *Journeys*

   index: _____ octopus: *Octopises*

▶▶ *Make a personal list of nouns, with an example for each category listed at the top of the page.*

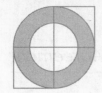

Parts of Speech
Pronouns

A **pronoun** is a word that takes the place of a noun or a group of words.

Here is a short list of common pronouns.

I, he, she, it, you, we, us, they, them, my, its, his, her, hers, our, ours, their, myself, himself, your, yourself, herself, itself, themselves

> Make sure the **pronouns** that are used in place of the nouns make sense. Also, don't overuse pronouns. Using too many can cause confusion for the reader, especially if he/she can't follow which nouns are being replaced by which pronouns.

1. Use **pronouns** from the list to complete these sentences. (Several different combinations are possible. Make sure the sentence makes sense after you add the pronouns.)

   (a) That car was ___his___, and ___he___ gave it to ___us___.

   (b) ___My___ team played as if ___we___ were playing ___our___ last game.

   (c) ___They___ liked it when ___I___ scored goals, and cheered when ___we___ won ___it___ all.

Another type of pronoun is the **indefinite pronoun**. It refers to a noun or pronoun that is not clearly named. Here are some indefinite pronouns.

another, anybody, anyone, anything, each, either, everybody, everyone, everything, much, neither, no one, nothing, one, other, somebody, someone, something, both, few, many, several, all, any, most, none, some

2. Use **indefinite pronouns** to complete these sentences.

   (a) ___everybody___ saw the thief creep out of the house with ___everything___

   (b) ___Both___ Cristine and Jon left ___everyone___ at the party wondering what had happened.

   (c) ___Something___ was not right with the situation, and ___no one___ knew how to fix the problem.

3. Write two sentences of your own using **indefinite pronouns**.

   (a) ___Is anyone free to do something ~~&~~ tomorrow.___

   (b) ___Most people no someone that has died.___

4. Other pronouns: **who, whoever, whomever, whose, what, whatever, which, that, this, these, those.** Use some of these pronouns in two sentences of your own.

   (a) ___Whoever broke the lamp that is in my room has to pay for it.___

   (b) ___What the hell is that flying in the sky.___

> ▶ *Try to write a piece that uses only pronouns instead of nouns. Does it make sense?*

Parts of Speech   *Noun, Pronoun Agreement*

A **pronoun** replaces or "agrees" with its **antecedent** or **the noun it is replacing**.

Joseph rows on the rowing team, and he thinks they will win the race.

(**Joseph** is the antecedent for **he**; **rowing team** is the antecedent for **they**.)

1. Indicate the **antecedent** for each pronoun in these sentences. Write them, with their pronouns, on the lines.

    (a) Jennifer watched as her sister tried to hit the ball as it was pitched toward her.

    _____

    (b) The truck hit its rear wheel against a curb, throwing the driver and his cargo out onto the ground.

    _____

    (c) "I wish we had tried harder," sighed Louise to her team.

    _____

    (d) The old tiger watched the hunters enter her territory, slinging their guns on their shoulders.

    _____

    (e) Without help, the entire crew would perish. They knew this as they sent Kyle to seek out the Ranger Station down the mountainside. "I can do this," he thought, "and everybody will be rescued. I just have to remember where we saw it as we flew over the valley."

    _____

    _____

2. Complete the story started in Activity #1(e). Write it as a **short paragraph**, telling what happens after Kyle leaves to get help. Use **pronouns** and **antecedents** in your paragraph. At the end of the paragraph, list the antecedents and their pronouns.

    _____

    _____

    _____

    _____

    _____

    _____

    _____

   How many pronouns can one antecedent have? Write a short piece on a topic of your choice, giving as many pronouns as you can for one antecedent. It has to sound right, and make sense. Good luck!

Parts of Speech
Verbs: Active/Passive Voice

The **active voice** shows that the subject **acts**: The player **hit** the ball.

The **passive voice** shows that the subject is **acted upon**: The ball **was hit** by the player.

> **Active** and **passive voice** verbs are both effective, depending on the context. Use either one when writing, as it fits your context. It's best to alter the use of the active and passive voice and not stay with one style or the other.

1. Rewrite each of these sentences in the **active voice**.

   (a) The car was hit by the truck.

   The car hit the truck.

   (b) The city was overrun by the storm.

   The storm overran the city.

   (c) The ships were loaded by the dock workers.

   _____

   (d) A joyous time was experienced by the tourists.

   _____

2. Rewrite each of these sentences in the **passive voice**.

   (a) The pilot radioed the tower for help.

   _____

   (b) Many students ordered chili that day.

   _____

   (c) They lost the race on a technicality.

   _____

   (d) Two dogs chased the cat up a tree.

   _____

3. Write a **short paragraph** on a topic of your choice. Use both **active** and **passive voice** in your sentences as appropriate.

   _____

   _____

   _____

   _____

   _____

   _____

   _____

 Check written materials for use of active and passive voice. Discover which type is more effective.

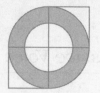

Parts of Speech

Verb tense shows the **time** of the action. The common verb tenses are: **past, present,** and **future.** Here are these verb tenses in context.
- **past:** I played the game.
- **present:** I play the game.
- **future:** I will play the game. I am going to play the game.

You can also give the present tense by using the **present participle** (verb form with **-ing**) and a form of the verb **to be**: I **am playing** the game.

> The **present tense** uses the base form of the verb, such as **play**, **shake**, **quiver**. The **past tense** adds **-ed** in most cases to the base form of the verb. The **future tense** uses the helper verb **will** or **shall** with the base form of the verb.

1. Rewrite each sentence, changing the verb from the **present tense** to the **past tense**, then to the **future tense**.

   (a) The crowd yells at the opposing team.

   past: _____

   future: _____

   (b) Everyone cheers the winning team.

   past: _____

   future: _____

   (c) The championship team parades around the field with the trophy.

   past: _____

   future: _____

2. Look at these verb tenses.

   - **present perfect:** She has played the game. (uses **has** or **have** and the **past participle** of the main verb)

   - **past perfect:** She had played the game. (uses **had** and the **past participle** of the main verb)

   - **future perfect:** She will have played the game. (uses **will** or **shall** with **have** and the **past participle** of the main verb)

   Write a sentence for each of these verb tenses using the example above.

   (a) **present perfect:**_____

   _____

   (b) **past perfect:** _____

   _____

   (c) **future perfect:** _____

   _____

 Select a short piece of writing, such as a song lyric. Rewrite it using a different verb tense than the original writing. How does this change the piece?

Parts of Speech

Transitive verbs: The action *goes across* to an object: The man **drives** *the car.*

Intransitive verbs: There is no object, but there may be modifiers: The man **drives** *fast.*

Copula verbs: The verb is completed by a subjective completion, which relates back to the subject: The driver **is** *a man.*

> **Transitive**—action goes across to object
> **Intransitive**—action is usually described, no object
> **Copula**—Completed by words relating back to subject

1. Tell whether the verb in each of the following is **transitive** or **intransitive**.

   (a) She refused his offer of a ride home. _____

   (b) She threw confetti at the wedding. _____

   (c) The teacher arranged the desks. _____

   (d) The students listened closely. _____

2. Rewrite each of the sentences in Activity #1, changing the verb from **transitive** to **intransitive**, or the reverse.

   (a) _____

   (b) _____

   (c) _____

   (d) _____

Copula verbs do not express action and are few in number. The most common ones are:

is   are   was   were   am   becomes   seems   taste   sound   smell

3. Circle the **copula verbs** and underline the **subjective completions** in each of the following:

   (a) The old dog is slow.

   (b) The melon tastes sweet.

   (c) These students seem diligent.

   (d) The grass is always greener...

4. Write sentences using the following verbs as **transitive**, **intransitive**, and **copula** verbs.

   a) turn

   transitive: _____

   intransitive: _____

   copula: _____

   b) grow

   transitive: _____

   intransitive: _____

   copula: _____

87

Parts of Speech   *Verbals: Infinitive, Gerund*

An **infinitive** is the base form of a verb, preceded by *to*, and used as a noun, adjective, or adverb.

To win is what the team must do.

> A **verbal** is a verb used as a part of speech other than a verb, such as a noun.

1. Underline the **infinitives** in these sentences.

    (a) The team wants to play on the new turf.

    (b) Whenever the sailor gets on board, he can't wait to sail out to sea.

    (c) It will be difficult to obtain another package of this sort, especially since we paid too much for it in the first place.

2. Write three sentences that use **infinitives**.

    (a) _____

    _____

    (b) _____

    _____

    (c) _____

    _____

A **gerund** is a verb form that is used as a noun and ends in **-ing**.

Running was his favourite pastime.

3. Use these gerunds to complete the sentences below.

    borrowing   swimming   joking

    (a) _____ the Great Lakes was a dream she had all of her life.

    (b) _____ money can be a difficult thing to manage.

    (c) _____ in front of an audience always relaxed him.

4. Write three sentences that use **gerunds**.

    (a) _____

    _____

    (b) _____

    _____

    (c) _____

    _____

> ▶ *Look for examples of infinitives and gerunds being used in everyday writing and speech. Keep a record of how often these verb forms come up in usage.*

Parts of Speech

Verbals: Participle

A **participle** is a verb form that can be used as an adjective. It can be **present** or **past**.

• **present participle:** Sharlene is a **captivating** speaker. (ends in **-ing**)

• **past participle:** Sharlene gave an **inspired** talk to the crowd, (usually ends in **-ed** or **-d**)

1. Give the **present** and **past participles** of these verbs.

    explain: _____, _____

    suggest: _____, _____

    recover: _____, _____

    apologize: _____, _____

    embarrass: _____, _____

    surprise: _____, _____

    guide: _____, _____

    irritate: _____, _____

    plummet: _____, _____

    budget: _____, _____

    entertain: _____, _____

    climb: _____, _____

2. Use **participles** from Activity #1 to complete these sentences. Make sure the sentences make sense when you add the participles!

    (a) The stock market was on a _____ trend for a week, but it soon regained its strength and was back in a _____ mode by Friday.

    (b) Jerold is in an _____ situation with his _____ verbal attack on Marci.

    (c) The _____ present for the party has been a _____ light in our planning.

3. Write a paragraph on a topic of your choice. Use at least six **participles** from those given in Activity #1. Underline the participles you use in your paragraph.

    _____

    _____

    _____

    _____

    _____

    _____

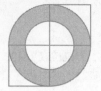

Parts of Speech

Use this page to practise your use of **verbals**: **infinitives**, **gerunds**, and **participles**.

Write an advertisement for a product, critique of a movie, poem, short story, or an opinion piece on a topic of your choice. Use verbals in your writing to add variety to your style. Don't overuse them, but try to make them integral to the meaning of your piece. At the end, indicate which type of verbals you used, listing them next to the verbal type.

_____

_____

_____

_____

_____

_____

_____

_____

_____

_____

_____

_____

_____

_____

_____

_____

_____

_____

_____

_____

_____

_____

Verbals used:

infinitives: _____

gerunds: _____

participles: _____

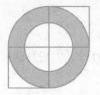

Parts of Speech

Adjectives and Phrases

An **adjective** is a word that describes a noun or pronoun.

The **sweltering** heat affected the group. (**Sweltering** is an adjective describing the noun **heat**.)

Adjectives can be:

> **Adjectives** answer to the questions **Which** or **What kind**. They are used to make writing more descriptive. Use them whenever you can to create a better picture in the mind of your reader.

• **determiners:** the, a, an;

• **proper:** South American, Canadian;

• **compound:** two-hour-long, seventy-fifth;

• **comparative:** happier, better, longer;

• **superlative:** happiest, best, longest.

1. Underline the **adjectives** in these sentences.

    (a) The shortest day was on a bright June 21st.

    (b) A happy couple jumped for joy as they won the ocean trip.

    (c) The twelve-day-long festival continued until the last trumpet blast.

2. Use **adjectives** to make these sentences more interesting. Rewrite the sentences with the adjectives.

    (a) The team won. _____

    _____

    (b) The baker worked hard. _____

    _____

    (c) The band played. _____

    _____

3. **Adjectives** can also be **phrases**: The popular singer **from Paris** caught the attention of the crowd. **Adjective phrases** start with **prepositions**. Underline the adjective phrases in these sentences.

    (a) The pilot of the airplane landed it safely.

    (b) A mark of success is the ability to try again.

    (c) The actor with makeup smeared called the director.

4. Write a short paragraph on a topic of your choice. Use **adjectives** and **adjective phrases** to make your writing more descriptive.

    _____

    _____

    _____

    _____

Parts of Speech

Adverbs and Phrases

An **adverb** is a word that describes a verb, an adjective, or another adverb.

> **Adverbs** answer the questions **How, When, Where, To what extent**. They can make your writing more descriptive.

The dog ran **quickly**. (**Quickly** describes the verb **ran**.)

Many adverbs are formed by adding **-ly** to an adjective: amazing: amazingly; slow: slowly.

1. Make **adverbs** from these **adjectives** by adding **-ly**. Check the spelling of your adverbs with a dictionary.

   wrong: _____   massive: _____

   efficient: _____   smart: _____

2. Use the **adverbs** in Activity #1 to complete these sentences.

   (a) We realized that he was _____ accused.

   (b) The player sent the ball _____ across the court.

   (c) She used her talents _____ as she fixed the broken water main.

   (d) We ran from the _____ moving fireball.

3. **Adverbs** can be **phrases**: We watched **from the top of the roof**. **Adverb phrases** start with **prepositions**. Underline the adverbs and adverb phrases in these sentences.

   (a) The driver turned his truck slowly into the ditch.

   (b) We gathered at the top to see the northern lights streak across the sky.

4. Use **adverbs** and **adverb phrases** to make these sentences more descriptive. Rewrite the sentences on the lines.

   (a) She did well. _____

   _____

   (b) The student council organized the dance. _____

   _____

5. Write a short paragraph on a topic of your choice. Use **adverbs** and **adverb phrases** to make your paragraph more descriptive.

   _____

   _____

   _____

   _____

   _____

 Check for adverb usage in published writings. List those that seem to be particularly creative.

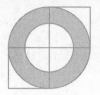

Sentences

Purposes

Sentences have four purposes:

- **declarative:** The campers pitched their tents. (makes a statement; ends with a period)

- **interrogative:** Where did the campers pitch their tents? (a question; ends with a question mark)

- **imperative:** Tell the campers to pitch their tents. (a command; the subject "you" is understood; can end with a period or exclamation mark)

- **exclamatory:** What a mess whenever campers pitch their tents! (a strong feeling is expressed; ends with an exclamation mark)

1. Identify the **purpose** of each sentence:

    (a) What did you think was going to happen if you didn't come to class? _____

    (b) I just hope we all have a safe trip down the Colorado River. _____

    (c) When did Jasmine say she was purchasing the tickets? _____

    (d) This room has to be cleaned up today! _____

    (e) Get me the owner of this company on the phone now! _____

    (f) Pass the salt. _____

2. Write one example for each **sentence purpose**. Identify the purpose at the end of the sentence.

    (a) _____

    _____

    (b) _____

    _____

    (c) _____

    _____

    (d) _____

    _____

3. Write a short paragraph that uses all four kinds of sentences. You may use a certain kind of sentence more than once to make your paragraph flow better.

    _____

    _____

    _____

    _____

 Try writing a short piece using only one kind of sentence, such as all interrogative. Does it make sense?

Sentences

Simple

A **simple sentence** has one **main clause** with a **subject** and a **predicate**.

The tiger wandered into the camp. (**The tiger** is the subject; **wandered into the camp** is the predicate.)

> The **subject** is **who** or **what** the sentence is about. The **predicate** is the **verb** of the sentence. It is what the subject does.

1. In each of these simple sentences, underline the **subject**. Put a wavy line under the **predicate**.

   (a) Warren caught the fastball out in left field.

   (b) Too many ticket holders crashed the gate to the concert.

   (c) A long line of trucks surrounded the government offices.

   (d) Frighteningly high waves pounded the sides of the cargo vessel.

2. Make **simple sentences** by adding **predicates** to these **subjects**.

   (a) The entire crowd_____

   (b) A very quiet hush_____

   (c) Many circus performers_____

   (d) The lightning _____

3. Make **simple sentences** by adding **subjects** to these **predicates**.

   (a) _____ watched the paint can roll off her ladder.

   (b) _____ stopped at every restaurant on the way home.

   (c) _____ followed the cat into the house.

   (d) _____ had always tried to win their games.

4. Write at least three simple sentences of your own. You may wish to put them together into paragraph form.

   _____

   _____

   _____

   _____

   _____

   _____

   _____

Read through a newspaper article. How many simple sentences were used? Does this type of sentence seem to be the most popular used by the author?

Sentences

Compound

A **compound sentence** has two or more **main clauses**. They are linked by a **conjunction** or a **semicolon**. Compound sentences are made from simple sentences.

The skier sped down the hill **and** he narrowly missed a tree. (This compound sentence is made from the two simple sentences **The skier sped down the hill** and **He narrowly missed a tree**. It is joined together with the conjunction **and**.)

1. Use **conjunctions** below to join each pair of **simple sentences** into **compound sentences**.

    and but or for yet

    (a) A tall package arrived yesterday. No one wanted to open it.

    _____

    (b) The motorcycle fell off the display. Everyone was startled.

    _____

    (c) Fifty tickets were left over. Blaine decided to purchase all of them.

    _____

2. **Compound sentences** can be joined by **semicolons**.

    The team ran onto the field; it was still a losing event.

    | Vary the use of **conjunctions** and **semicolons** when making **compound sentences**. Don't rely on just one method. |

    Use **semicolons** to join these **simple sentences** to form **compound sentences**.

    (a) People tried to pull the rocks aside. It was a great effort.

    _____

    (b) The car stopped quickly. Everyone poured out onto the street.

    _____

    (c) A balloon carried the weather instruments aloft. We knew it would work.

    _____

3. Write a short paragraph on a topic of your choice that uses a mixture of **simple sentences** and **compound sentences**. Use at least two compound sentences in your paragraph.

    _____

    _____

    _____

    _____

    _____

    _____

 Select a piece of writing from a newspaper or magazine. Look for simple sentences that could be combined into compound sentences. Rewrite the piece with compound sentences. Is the writing improved?

Sentences

Complex

A **complex sentence** has one **main clause** and one or more **subordinate clauses**.

As he drove away, Milton could see the crowd in his mirror.

(subordinate clause)   (main clause)

> A **main clause** can stand on its own as a sentence.
> A **subordinate clause** cannot stand on its own as a sentence, even though it has a subject and a predicate.

1. Add **subordinate clauses** to these **main clauses** to make **complex sentences**.

    (a) The day began slowly _____

    (b) We had to climb above the stands _____

    _____

    (c) _____

    _____, she saw the accident.

    (d) Blair worked at the convenience store _____

    _____

2. Add **main clauses** to these **subordinate clauses** to make **complex sentences**.

    (a) After trying to get his friend on the phone,_____

    _____

    (b) When the band began to play their hit song,_____

    _____

    (c) After the hurricane struck the coast, and when the people had evacuated their homes,

    _____

    (d) As the wind grew in intensity,_____

    _____

3. Write a short paragraph on a topic of your choice. Use **complex sentences** as the main type of sentences in your paragraph.

    _____

    _____

    _____

    _____

    _____

    _____

    _____

    _____

 Find examples of complex sentences in everyday material. Look for ways of creating complex sentences in your own writing as well.

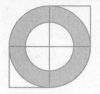

Sentences

Compound-Complex

A **compound-complex sentence** has two or more **main clauses** and one or more **subordinate clauses**.

After the crew had cleaned up, the band left the arena and they boarded their bus.

(subordinate clause)   (main clause)   (main clause)

1. Add **subordinate clauses** to these **main clauses** to make **compound-complex sentences**.

   (a) _____

   _____, the singer stopped singing and she turned to look at the audience.

   (b) _____

   _____, she realized that the concert was ruined and her career was in doubt.

   (c) _____

   _____, her lawyer advised against suing, but she did suggest that some legal action was necessary.

2. Add **main clauses** to these **subordinate clauses** to make **compound-complex sentences**.

   (a) After their agreement had expired, _____

   _____

   (b) Whenever the crew set up the stage, _____

   _____

   (c) _____

   _____ as the show started on time.

3. Select one of the following ideas. Write a selection using **compound-complex sentences** as the major type of sentence.

   advertising copy for a new product   a poem   a description of an event

   _____

   _____

   _____

   _____

   _____

   _____

   _____

 Try to write a short piece using only compound-complex sentences. Does the writing sound proper?

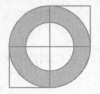

Sentences

This page will give you practice in various **sentence types** and **purposes**.

Write a sample on a topic of your choice. It could be an advertisement, a story, an article similar to that found in a newspaper, a journal entry, a poem, and so on. Use a variety of sentence types: **simple**, **compound**, **complex**, and **compound-complex**. Use all four sentence purposes: **declarative**, **interrogative**, **imperative**, and **exclamatory**. Good writing!

_____

_____

_____

_____

_____

_____

_____

_____

_____

_____

_____

_____

_____

_____

_____

_____

_____

_____

_____

_____

_____

_____

_____

_____

_____

 Use what you wrote on this page as a rough draft. Rewrite the selection in good copy after checking it. Present the good copy to an audience of your choice.

Sentences

Clauses: Main and Subordinate

A **clause** is a group of words that contains a **subject** and a **predicate** (verb).

There are two types of clauses:

> Every **sentence** is made up of **clauses**. Each sentence has at least a main clause. Many sentences have both **main** and **subordinate clauses**. Subordinate clauses can be **noun clauses**, **adjective clauses**, or **adverb clauses**.

• **main clause:** can stand on its own as a sentence: **The heat continued all day.**

• **subordinate clause:** cannot stand on its own as a sentence: **After the rain drenched the city**

1. Identify each of these as a **main** or a **subordinate clause**.

    (a) The team went into its practice. _____

    (b) As they were getting ready to go, _____

    (c) After helping the earthquake victims, _____

2. Write a **main clause** for each **subordinate clause** to make complete sentences.

    (a) When they finished the stage set, _____

    _____

    (b) After Clive set the timing on his motorcycle, _____

    _____

    (c) _____

    _____ which will fly farther than any craft before it.

3. Write a **subordinate clause** for each **main clause** to make complete sentences.

    (a) He finally entered the room, _____

    _____

    (b) _____

    _____, the car swerved out of control.

4. Write two sentences on topics of your choice that use **main** and **subordinate clauses** in each.

    (a) _____

    _____

    (b) _____

    _____

 Find examples of main clauses in everyday writing. Add subordinate clauses to them. Does this improve the meaning of the sentences?

Usage Problems

Sentence Fragments

Remember: A **sentence** must have a **subject** and a **predicate** (verb). If one of these is not present, the group of words is a **sentence fragment**. It cannot stand as a sentence.

1. Identify each of these as **sentence** or **sentence fragment**.

   (a) The mill in the town shut down after fifty years of operation. _____

   (b) Many workers who toiled at the plant. _____

   (c) A severance package was granted to each employee. _____

   (d) The plant owners. _____

   (e) My uncle worked there for thirty years. _____

   Rewrite the **sentence fragments** that you identified as full sentences.

   _____

   _____

   _____

   _____

   _____

2. Read this paragraph. Underline any **sentence fragment** you find. Rewrite the sentence fragments correctly.

   We travelled all night, looking for the resort. Finally, it loomed out of the fog. The lights. Our exhaustion. We knew we had little time. We had to get inside. For days before our trip. This was to be our refuge.

   _____

   _____

   _____

   _____

3. Some **sentence fragments** can be used effectively, such as in advertisements. Look at this example: **The thrills! The spills! The RIDE! Come to *Wonder Park* for the RIDE of a lifetime!** Sentence fragments at the beginning of the ad set the tone for the ad and give information in a quick way. Write a short advertisement that uses a mixture of **sentences** and **sentence fragments** effectively.

   _____

   _____

   _____

   _____

 Find examples of sentence fragments in everyday usage. Check their effectiveness.

Usage Problems

Run-on sentences happen when two or more main clauses are written together without breaks: **The plane taxied down the runway it took off on time**. This should be broken into two sentences: **The plane taxied down the runway. It took off on time**.
Run-on sentences can be fixed by:

- **rewriting them as two sentences:** The plane taxied down the runway. It took off on time.

- **using punctuation and rewording if necessary:** The plane taxied down the runway; it took off on time.

- **making one clause subordinate and rewording if necessary:** The plane taxied down the runway **as it took off on time**.

- **adding a co-ordinating conjunction:** The plane taxied down the runway **and** it took off on time.

1. Fix these **run-on sentences** using one of the methods described above.

    (a) Jeremy tried on his new team jacket he was proud to wear it.

    _____

    (b) The convoy of trucks encircled the offices they were protesting the new contract.

    _____

A **comma splice** happens when two main clauses are joined by a comma:

The workers finished for the day, they went off to their families. This problem can be fixed similar to the run-on sentence problem. The easiest way is to eliminate the commas and rewrite as two sentences: **The workers finished for the day. They went off to their families**.

2. Fix these **comma splices** using methods similar to those for run-on sentences.

    (a) A wayward tire rolled down the hill, it signalled a concern up ahead.

    _____

    (b) Too few volunteers showed up for the concert, we were quite disappointed.

    _____

3. Rewrite this paragraph correcting **run-on sentence** and **comma splice** problems.

    The top of the tower came into view, it was clearly taller than any building around the architect had tried to reach new heights. We knew what was on her mind when she designed it she was trying to show how great her engineering skills were we saw it as a colossal ego trip.

    _____

    _____

    _____

    _____

Usage Problems

Subject-Verb Agreement

Subjects and **verbs** must **agree in number**. Singular subjects take singular verbs. Plural subjects take plural verbs.

> Look for the **subject**, not words describing it, when you want to check for agreement.

1. Circle the **correct verb** in the parentheses **that agrees with the subject** in each sentence.

    (a) The team (has won, have won) enough games to enter the playoffs.

    (b) A committee of elected officials (debate, debates) the issues at 9:00 tonight.

    (c) All of the tea (is, are) gone, and we (has, have) nothing left to drink.

    (d) The class (play, plays) a form of Trivial Pursuit on Mondays.

    (e) Measles (is, are) a very unpleasant disease.

2. Use these verbs in sentences. Make sure the **subjects agree** with them.

    (a) hovers: _____

    _____

    (b) drive: _____

    _____

    (c) scatters: _____

    _____

    (d) stops: _____

    _____

    (e) exaggerates: _____

    _____

3. Write a paragraph on a topic of your choice. Make sure that your **subjects** and **verbs** **agree**.

    _____

    _____

    _____

    _____

    _____

    _____

    _____

    _____

    _____

 Check song lyrics, and other material that you may come in contact with during the day. Look for correct subject-verb agreement. Correct any that you may find as being incorrect.

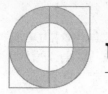

Usage Problems

A **misplaced modifier** is a modifier that is in a misleading location in the sentence. It sounds as if it is modifying the wrong thing: **Standing at the crease, the puck passed by the goalie.** The modifier, **standing at the crease**, describes **where** the goalie was standing. In the sentence, it looks like **standing at the crease** is describing **the puck**! The sentence should read: **The puck passed by the goalie standing at the crease**.

1. Fix these sentences with **misplaced modifiers** by rewriting them with the modifiers near the words being modified.

   (a) Crouching low in the brush, the mouse walked by the cat.

   _____

   (b) Singing at the top of her lungs, the piano was played by Shirley.

   _____

   (c) To get a ticket to the concert, the credit card was used by Dwayne.

   _____

   (d) Many people use chemicals on crops that are dangerous to the environment.

   _____

A **dangling modifier** is unclear in what it is modifying: **Having won the trial race, the marathon didn't concern Philippe**. This can be corrected by placing the modifier next to the words it is modifying: **Having won the trial race, Philippe wasn't concerned about the marathon**. Notice that some words were changed to make the sentence flow smoothly.

2. Rewrite these sentences, correcting the **dangling modifiers**.

   (a) Watching the eagles soar, the mountainside was climbed by Elise.

   _____

   (b) Hearing the news, the play was shifted by the team.

   _____

   (c) Discouraged by terrible passes, quitting the game became an option.

   _____

3. Rewrite these ads fixing any **modifier problems**.

   For Sale: A slightly used sailboat for ocean fishing with newer masts

   _____

   Available Now! Pairs of pants, plenty of shirts with ripped knees

   _____

 Read through some ads or other everyday writings, looking for modifier problems. Rewrite them fixing any problems found.

Usage Problems

Split Infinitives, Double Negatives

A **split infinitive** happens when a **modifier** is placed between **to** and the **verb form**: to **loudly** whisper. It is best to avoid this type of problem and rewrite the modifier out of the infinitive: to whisper **loudly**.

> **Split infinitives** should not be used in formal English. They often come up in conversation, but they are not correct usage. Make sure that you do not use split infinitives in your writing.

1. Rewrite these **split infinitives**, placing the modifiers correctly.

   (a) to softly sing: _____   (b) to playfully laugh: _____

2. Rewrite these sentences, fixing any **split infinitives** that you find.

   (a) Peter was sure to effortlessly push the rock into the driveway, blocking the entrance to the house.

   _____

   _____

   (b) We are very happy to graciously accept this award on behalf of those who want to generously give us a chance in the music field.

   _____

   _____

A **double negative** happens when two negatives are put together in the same sentence: **I won't go to no movie**. To correct this, change the negative that deserves less impact to a neutral form: **I won't go to any movie**.

> A **double negative** is incorrect usage and language. It really means the opposite of what the speaker wants to say: **I won't go to no movies**, really means **I will go to all movies**. The speaker just wants to say **I won't go to any movies**, but the double negative gives an unclear impression.

3. Rewrite these sentences correcting any double negatives.

   (a) We haven't had no rain for weeks. _____

   (b) Jule wanted nothing to do with none of them. _____

   _____

4. Rewrite this paragraph correcting any **split infinitives** and **double negatives**.

   The horse galloped to easily catch the rest of the herd. It hadn't been with none of its kind for weeks. Finally, with great effort, it ran to quickly be beside the leader, not knowing no outcome of what would happen.

   _____

   _____

   _____

   _____

   _____

 Check for these usage problems, not only in writing, but in everyday speech. Pay particular attention to your use of language in formal situations.

CHECK UP 1 ▸ *Parts of Speech*

1. Define what a **noun** is. _____

2. What is the difference between a **common noun** and a **proper noun**? _____

   _____

3. Tell what an **antecedent** is in relation to **pronouns**. _____

   _____

4. In this sentence, write the **pronouns** and their **antecedents**.

   The teacher gave the test, but she forgot to mark it for the class. _____

   _____

5. **Adjectives** describe _____

   Adverbs describe _____

6. Rewrite these sentences adding interesting **adjectives** and **adverbs**.

   (a) The boat reached land._____

   _____

   (b) A jet broke the sound barrier. _____

   _____

7. Indicate whether each verb in these sentences is in the **active** or **passive voice**.

   (a) We rowed to the other shore. _____

   (b) The float was pulled by a tractor in the parade. _____

   (c) A car struck the telephone pole. _____

   (d) The test was passed by over half the class. _____

8. (a) For each of these verb **infinitives**, give its **past**, **present**, and **future tense**.

   to drive: _____

   to give: _____

   to chuckle: _____

   to be: _____

   (b) Select one of the verbs. Write a sentence using the verb in any of the three tenses.

   _____

   _____

1. What is a **verbal**? _____

   _____

2. Identify the **verbals** in these sentences as **participle**, **gerund**, or **infinitive**.

   (a) Laughing relaxed everyone's muscles. _____

   (b) Delaney was a droning talker. _____

   (c) The storyteller was happy to tell a story. _____

3. Use each of these **participles** in a sentence correctly as a **verbal**.

   entertaining: _____

   _____

   laughing: _____

   _____

   swarming: _____

   _____

4. Use each of these **gerunds** in a sentence correctly as a **verbal**.

   shoeing: _____

   _____

   acting: _____

   _____

   sighting: _____

   _____

5. Use each of these **infinitives** in a sentence correctly as a **verbal**.

   to create: _____

   _____

   to rescue: _____

   _____

   to view: _____

   _____

6. Write a sentence using any type of **verbal**. Identify what kind of verbal you used at the end of your sentence.

   _____

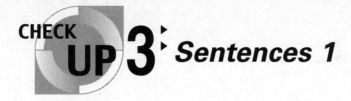

1. Give the four **sentence purposes** and a brief description of each.

   (a) _____ : _____

   (b) _____ : _____

   (c) _____ : _____

   (d) _____ : _____

2. In these sentences, draw a line between the **subject** and the **predicate**.

   (a) The lonely musician played long into the night.

   (b) Many in the audience heard his plaintive notes echoing into the room.

   (c) A call came after midnight to close for the day.

   (d) He played after they had left, not wanting to go home.

3. What is the difference between a **main clause** and a **subordinate clause**? _____

   _____

4. Underline the **main clauses** in these sentences. Bracket the **subordinate clauses**.

   (a) After completing the work in the storeroom, Jillian walked back to the storefront.

   (b) Her day had been a triumph because it was a great experience to organize the stock.

   (c) Whenever she could do it, Jillian went into the stockroom to check on her work.

5. Write **main clauses** for these **subordinate clauses** to make complete sentences.

   (a) After the eclipse had ended, _____

   _____

   (b) _____, whenever he called us by name.

   (c) _____ who want to participate in the game _____

   _____

6. Write three sentences on topics of your choice. Each sentence is to have a **main clause** and a **subordinate clause**. You may wish to put the sentences together as a paragraph.

   _____

   _____

   _____

   _____

   _____

   _____

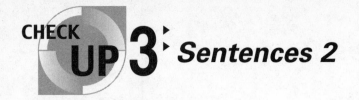

1. What is a **simple sentence**? _____

    _____

    Write an example of a simple sentence. _____

    _____

2. What is a **compound sentence**? _____

    _____

    Write an example of a compound sentence. _____

    _____

3. What is a **complex sentence**? _____

    _____

    Write an example of a complex sentence. _____

    _____

4. What is a **compound-complex sentence**? _____

    _____

    Write an example of a compound-complex sentence. _____

    _____

5. Write a paragraph on a topic of your choice. Use examples of each type of sentence listed in Activities #1 to #4. Use a variety of sentences to make your paragraph interesting.

    _____

    _____

    _____

    _____

    _____

    _____

    _____

    _____

    _____

    _____

    _____

1. Check this paragraph for **sentence fragments**. Rewrite the paragraph with the fragments corrected.

   The day of our practice. We hadn't thought about the opposition. Were they well-grouped? Did they? We hadn't a clue as to what to think. The game. It was to be next week. Prepared? Were we?

   _____

   _____

   _____

   _____

2. Rewrite these **run-on sentences** as proper sentences.

   (a) The time of our victory was here we had nowhere to celebrate.

   _____

   (b) A little drop of acid fell onto the floor it ate through the metal like it was paper.

   _____

   (c) More than the crowd booed the players many band members sneered at the stars.

   _____

3. Rewrite these **comma splices** as proper sentences.

   (a) The train swept into the tunnel, it headed straight for the distant opening.

   _____

   (b) Thousands crammed into the square, he turned to look at them.

   _____

   (c) A little light went on in her head, the day could be salvaged after all.

   _____

4. Rewrite this paragraph fixing any **subject-verb agreement** problems.

   His first driving test are going to be an adventure. He put on the brakes too soon, and the tester frown at him like he had never see a car before. Finally, after much trying, he shift the gear and the car pull out of the parking lot with the tester holding his head tightly, not wanting to looks out the window.

   _____

   _____

   _____

   _____

   _____

1. Describe two **modifier problems** that can be found in writing. _____

   _____

   _____

2. Rewrite these sentences fixing any **modifier problems**.

   (a) Having jumped above the fence, the ball sailed past the catcher's glove.

   _____

   (b) Being afraid of nothing, the wind whipped at Jessica's face.

   _____

   (c) She sold a car to a friend with transmission problems.

   _____

   (d) The principal called the student into her office with a missed detention.

   _____

3. Fix the **split infinitives** in these sentences. Rewrite the corrected sentences.

   (a) The time to rightly claim our prize is upon us!

   _____

   (b) A truly imaginative socket wrench was found to lately be attached too long to the machine.

   _____

   (c) Henry yelled that he was to boldly find his way out of the maze.

   _____

   (d) Her mathematics test was to creatively invest in the stock market and to ruthlessly make more money than she had invested.

   _____

   _____

4. Rewrite these sentences, fixing any **double negatives** that you find.

   (a) We won't go to no hockey games when they don't play no good!

   _____

   (b) I haven't seen no deer in this area since they can't come to no place for food.

   _____

   (c) Maria never goes to no shows during the week, and doesn't like none of our choices.

   _____

   (d) The end is never better than the beginning and no beginning is never better than the end.

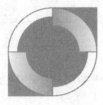

Unit 5

Putting It Together!

FOCUS ON: Writing

1. What are the steps in the **writing process**?

   _____

   _____

2. What does it mean when one **writes for an audience**?

   _____

   _____

3. What is the difference between a **narrative paragraph** and a **descriptive paragraph**?

   _____

   _____

4. What are the main parts of an **essay**?

   _____

   _____

5. What is a **thesis statement**?

   _____

   _____

6. Describe some differences between **formal writing** and **informal writing**.

   _____

   _____

7. How is an **editorial** an example of **opinion writing**?

   _____

   _____

8. What are other examples of **opinion writing**?

   _____

   _____

9. What are some **poetic forms** used by poets?

   _____

   _____

10. How is a **short story** different from a **novel**, other than its length?

   _____

   _____

The **writing process** often is made up of five steps:

- **prethinking:** getting ideas, brainstorming, finding information

- **drafting:** putting the ideas into written form for the first time

- **revising:** going over the first draft to rethink words, ideas, structure

- **editing/proofreading:** checking the work for grammatical, spelling, mechanical errors and revising

- **publishing/presenting:** producing the work in its final, good copy for others to read

> Not every type of writing requires the **writing process**. Journal and diary writing is done *as is* by the author, without changes. Also, the five steps listed may not necessarily be used every time: a great first draft with editing may be all that is needed for some pieces of writing. It is best to go over every piece of writing carefully, with the idea that **creating the best possible final copy is the goal.**

Use the writing process for most of the formal writing that you do.

On this page, write down how you use the writing process, or some form of it, when you write. What do you do when you write an assignment, or a story? How do you get your ideas? When do you revise your work? When do you consider your audience as you write? Is there ever a time when what you write originally is *it*? Use these questions to guide you as you respond.

_____

_____

_____

_____

_____

_____

_____

_____

_____

_____

_____

_____

 Select a piece of writing from an everyday source, such as a newspaper. Indicate how much of the writing process you feel the author used. For example, a reported news story may use a draft only with some editing due to time factors.

Putting It Together!

The first step in writing is getting an idea. **Ideas** can come from many sources:

- talking to friends and relatives;
- remembering past experiences;
- using your imagination;
- researching other sources and information;
- reviewing previous ideas you may have had.

- interviewing;
- brainstorming;

> Keep an **ideas folder** or **writer's notebook**. Write any ideas down that you think might make a good story or informative piece later. Think of this as a topics folder and a place for inspiration!

1. These methods for generating ideas are not the only ones. Think about what you do when you are asked to write something. What methods are familiar to you when you want to generate an idea?

   _____

   _____

   _____

2. How do you get ideas when you have to write an **essay**, or other type of **informative writing**?

   _____

   _____

   _____

3. What do you do to generate ideas for **creative writing**, such as **poems** or **short stories**?

   _____

   _____

4. Your teacher has assigned a history piece to be written. What are some **history writings** that could be done? List them here.

   _____

   _____

   _____

5. A poetry anthology has been assigned to be written by members of the English class. What types of **poetic writing** could go into this? List your ideas here.

   _____

   _____

   _____

 Think of something you would really like to write. Where do you get your ideas for this?

Putting It Together! *Gathering Information*

Once you have an idea for a piece of writing, the next step is to gather information.

Gathering information is similar to generating ideas. You can gather information by:

> Keep a **journal of ideas** that can be used when you write a piece. Jot ideas down, no matter how insignificant they may seem at the time. You never know when a bit of information can become useful!

• reading through printed sources, such as books, newspapers, and magazines;

• talking to friends and relatives about your topic and what you need for information;

• interviewing people who may have the information you seek;

• reviewing material that you had gathered previously;

• viewing videos, films, or listening to sources such as CDs and tapes.

1. How do you gather information for an **informative piece**, such as an essay?

   _____

   _____

   _____

2. How do you gather information for a **creative piece**, such as a poem or short story?

   _____

   _____

   _____

3. Once you have gathered your information, how do you **organize** it?

   _____

   _____

   _____

4. You have been asked to write a report/article on the millennium celebrations that took place on January 1, 2000. What information would you need to gather? List some ideas about where you would get the information.

   _____

   _____

   _____

   _____

   _____

   _____

   _____

 Write a rough draft of the article outlined in Activity #4. Don't forget to include information from a variety of sources.

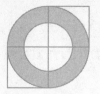

Putting It Together! *Selecting an Audience*

Writing must have a **purpose**. That purpose can range from writing for an assignment to writing for yourself. Whenever you write, you need to keep your **audience** in mind. That will determine what and how you write.

> An **audience** is anyone who reads written material, or who listens or views material. You can be an audience, just as a larger group can be one. Writers must always be aware of who their audience is before writing or creating.

1. Who might be potential **audiences** for these writings?

   (a) a prescription written by a doctor:_____

   (b) a song lyric by a rock group: _____

   (c) an article in the newspaper on government spending:_____

   (d) a poem written by a student:_____

   (e) a manual on fixing automobiles:_____

   (f) a recipe for a breakfast dish: _____

   (g) a listing of television programs: _____

   (h) a science textbook: _____

2. Some audiences require **formal writing**. Others can be presented with **informal writing**. An example of this would be e-mail or letters written to a friend. This would be informal in style. Make a list of types of writing and their potential audiences under the following headings.

   Formal Writing: _____

   _____

   _____

   _____

   Informal Writing: _____

   _____

   _____

   _____

3. You have been asked to write the following items. List **audiences** for whom you would write the pieces.

   (a) a geography essay on the impact of glaciers in Canada: _____

   _____

   (b) a short story on a disastrous concert: _____

   _____

   (c) a poem on what you believe in:_____

   _____

   (d) a résumé for a job at a local sports store:_____

   _____

▶▶ *Look for examples of writings that you feel were directed at the wrong audiences.*

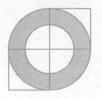

Putting It Together!

Voice and Language
in Writing

When writing, always be aware of what **voice** (active or passive) and **language** (formal or informal) you use. Both voice and language can be effective when used creatively. Overdoing either one can lead to dull writing that your audience will not stay with.

> For a review of the **active** and **passive voice**, see page 85. For a review of **formal** and **informal language**, see pages 47 and 48.

1. The following piece of writing uses **active voice** only and is given in **formal writing**. Rewrite it using a mixture of active and passive voice, and formal and informal language.

   The player hits the ball to left field. A left-fielder catches the ball and throws it back to the catcher just as a runner steals to home plate.
   "Out!" yells the umpire. At this point, the home side erupts in the dugout. The manager races across the field and stands nose-to-nose with the umpire.
   "You would not know an 'out' if you saw one!" he yells at the top of his lungs. The crowd behind the umpire boos incessantly, cheering as the manager berates him.
   "You are out of here!" the umpire yells back. Two players hold the manager back from going after the umpire.
   "I am not finished with you yet!" the manager replied in a harsh tone. The umpire turns and ignores him.

   _____

   _____

   _____

   _____

   _____

   _____

   _____

   _____

   _____

   _____

   _____

   _____

2. Write a short continuation of the story in Activity #1. Use a mixture of **active** and **passive voice**, and **informal** and **formal language**.

   _____

   _____

   _____

   _____

   _____

   _____

   _____

 Which style do you prefer: active? passive? formal? informal? Why?

Putting It Together!   *Paragraphs: Make-Up*

Successful paragraphs are clear in form and meaning to the reader. A **paragraph** usually has three characteristics:

- **unity:** the paragraph stays with one topic and doesn't stray in idea;

- **coherence:** the ideas in the paragraph progress logically within the paragraph;

- **emphasis:** the important ideas in the paragraph are evident to the reader.

> Make sure that your **paragraphs** always follow one topic at a time. They also need to have a logical sequencing of sentences within the paragraph itself (this means that one idea or sentence flows logically into the next one).

A good paragraph has a **topic sentence** that expresses the main idea. The topic sentence could be placed anywhere in the paragraph. After this, the rest of the sentences follow a logical sequence, presenting the information. At the end, a **clinching sentence** is given that sums up and sometimes adds to the main idea of the paragraph.

1. Rewrite these sentences in their proper order to create a paragraph. Underline the **topic sentence**.

    They tried to get to the door before it closed.
    Suddenly, the light from the doorway began to dim.
    The explorers had reached the secret chamber unharmed.
    Slowly, they entered the dusty room, looking about, their torches casting their shadows on the walls.

    _____

    _____

    _____

    _____

    _____

    _____

2. Select one of these topic sentences. Write a **short paragraph** that goes with the topic sentence. Remember: the topic sentence could be placed anywhere in the paragraph, as long as it makes sense.

    (a) The banker walked into his office.

    (b) Wildly, the racers entered the raceway, ready for a showdown to the finish.

    (c) We stayed all night in the old mansion, aware of the legend surrounding it.

    (d) At last, we reached the mountain's summit!

    _____

    _____

    _____

    _____

    _____

    _____

 Continue your story from Activity #2 with at least three other paragraphs.

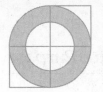

Putting It Together!

Essay: Form

Essays have a particular form when they are written:

• **introduction:** states the main idea (thesis) of the essay;

• **body:** develops the thesis of the essay following patterns of organization, such as

— *definition*: defines a key term (such as heroism) then clarifies and expands on this
— *comparison*: explores similarities and differences between things
— *cause and effect*: looks at reasons for events, such as "How do tornadoes form?"
— *problem-solution*: states a problem, with solutions clearly laid out and supported with facts and evidence, with the writer recommending a solution at the essay's end

• **conclusion:** a brief summary of the essay's main points, often with the writer's views on the topic.

> Select the **form** of your essay's body so that it suits what your essay is to be about. Make your **thesis statement** strong and clear so that the reader knows exactly what the essay is about.

1. Write a **thesis statement** for an essay you might write on one of these topics.
    **fairness in sports   a dream for the future   government's responsibilities
    men and women's roles**

    _____

    _____

    _____

2. In point form, write some ideas that would appear in the **body** of your essay based on your thesis statement from Activity #1.

    _____

    _____

    _____

    _____

    _____

    _____

    _____

    _____

3. Write some ideas that should be included in your **conclusion** to your essay from Activities #1 and #2.

    _____

    _____

    _____

    _____

    _____

    _____

 Write a rough draft of the essay you have partially planned on this page.

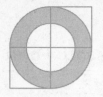

Informative Writing

Essay: Purpose

There are many reasons why we write essays. Quite simply, they are persuasive pieces of writing that present a point of view. Often, the point of view is gathered from information presented in the essay, but it always contains the author's views and feeling on the topic. The reader should know what the author's point of view is at the end of the essay.

> An **essay** does not have to be long. Some of the best essays are short and to the point. What must be kept in mind is the ability to stay on topic and not wander into other areas. Also, some essays will include the author's opinion in a subtle way, making it such a part of the essay that the reader sees the entire essay as the author's opinion, and not just one part.

Essay **purposes** can also be gathered from their types:

• **expository:** gives information about an event or issue, trying to explain features about the topic, such as a magazine article on a rock group;

• **narrative:** tells the story of an event or an experience, such as an author relating a trip;

• **reflective:** explores an idea or opinion about the world or some other large topic, such as a philosopher might do on the questions of life and death;

• **descriptive:** describes an event, person, place, or process, such as a character sketch;

• **persuasive:** attempts to win the reader over to a particular point of view, such as an editorial.

1. For each essay topic, write one of the five **essay types** that would best reflect how the essay should be written.

   (a) an essay on an actor and the roles she has played: _____

   (b) an essay telling about a group of mountain climbers and their experiences: _____

   (c) an essay talking about life in the Universe: _____

   (d) an essay presenting ideas about why guns need to be controlled: _____

   (e) an essay telling about the features in a new office building: _____

2. Use the rest of this page to begin writing a short essay on a topic of your choice. Select one of the essay types and identify which type your essay follows. Finish your essay on another sheet of paper.

   _____

   _____

   _____

   _____

   _____

   _____

   _____

   _____

   _____

 Find an example of a good essay. Read through it to see what catches your attention.

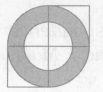

Informative Writing

A **speech** gives you a chance to let others hear your ideas. Speeches can be

Know the audience you are going to speak to. This will help you determine whether you will give a formal or informal speech.

- **formal:** a prepared talk on a subject, often involving research; cue cards are used, or the speech is memorized;

- **informal:** also called *impromptu* as the speaker shares ideas with little preparation; answering a question in class can be a short impromptu speech.

Use this page to **plan a speech** that you could give to an audience.

1. What are you interested in talking about? Write down as many **ideas** as you can.

   _____

   _____

   _____

   Now, select one **topic** that you would like to speak about. _____

2. What kind of a speech will this be: **formal** or **informal**? _____

3. Who will the **audience** be? _____

4. What **research** do you need to do? _____

   _____

5. What are some items or ideas you wish to say in your speech?

   _____

   _____

   _____

6. Write the beginning of a short **introduction** for your speech.

   _____

   _____

   _____

   Think of a way to **catch the attention** of your audience. Begin with a question, a joke (if it fits your speech), or anything that relates to your topic. This will help get your audience interested in your topic and they will be ready to listen intently to your speech.

7. Think of your speech's **conclusion**. How will you end your speech? Write the beginning of a possible ending here, wrapping up your ideas for the audience.

   _____

   _____

   _____

▶ *Write your speech out in full, then give it to the audience you selected.*

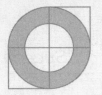

Informative Writing

Written correspondence with other people includes

- **letters:** writings that can be personal, such as to a friend or relative, or for business, such as to a company; a letter follows a specific format;

- **e-mail:** stands for *electronic mail* and is accomplished with a computer as a means of communicating with others.

Look at these three examples of correspondence.

Business letter

133 Grand Street
Delia, AB
T0J 1W5

> Heading

April 23, 2001

> Date

Ms. Halle Habib
Manager
Socrates Lab
81 North Avenue
Delia, AB
T0J 0W3

> Inside Address (the name and address of the person or organization to whom you are writing)

Dear Ms. Habib:

> Salutation

I would like to thank you for sending samples of your new candy to our class for testing. I can assure you that the taste-test part of my project was a success! The results of my experiment will be shared with you shortly.

> Body of the Letter

Thank you again for your assistance in my work.

Yours truly,
Elliott Wiston

> Complimentary Close

> Signature

Personal letter

May 18, 2001

Dear Joan,

How have you been? I hear your family will be visiting my area soon. Tell them to drop in when they get here—Mom and Dad would love to talk over old times!

Sincerely yours,

Johanne

E-mail

☐	Your Letter	▣▣

Send Address Attach Reply Reply All Forward Store Print Delete   ☐ Log ☐ Receipt
Normal ▼

X-Sender: 7pfb@qlink.queensu.ca
Date: Sat, Nov. 21, 1998 19:10:55-0500
To: ckarr@calvin.stemnet.mf.ca
From: Julie Romano <7pfb.@qlink.queensu.ca>
Subject: Your Letter

1 Item   317 Bytes

Text_1

What's with the snail mail, Cheryl? Join the electronic revolution! It was great to hear from you. I'm glad the music worked out.

I've been <u>incredibly</u> busy so far this term. Every prof thinks there's nothing to life but work, work, WORK.

It's amazing that I can do anything considering the quality of food here in the dorm. It is **SO BAD**! I'm sure missing those brownies we used to make. Hint, hint.

Tutorial time. Gotta go. Miss ya. Write soon.

Julie

P.S. Tell Kim I want more than "Hi" from her. Like an e-mail, maybe?

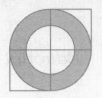

Informative Writing

Use this page to practise writing **correspondence**.

1. Write a short **business letter** to a company requesting information on a topic of your choice. You can use an actual company that you know, or make up the company and its address.

_____

_____

_____

_____

_____

_____

_____

_____

_____

_____

_____

_____

_____

2. Write the text for a short **e-mail message**, or a **personal letter** to a friend on a topic of your choice. Remember that e-mails and personal letters are more informal in their language, almost conversational.

_____

_____

_____

_____

_____

_____

_____

_____

_____

_____

_____

_____

_____

_____

 Look at examples of letters from other eras to see how people corresponded long ago.

Informative Writing

Editorial

An **editorial** is an opinion piece of writing that usually appears in a newspaper or a magazine. It gives the point of view or the official stand taken by the publication on a topic. Good editorials try to convince the reader of their viewpoints. Formal language is used; those that employ informal tones and words usually are seen as being reactionary or poorly written. Look at this example.

In a time of instant communication, it is a wonder that four days elapsed before the public were made aware of the dangers lurking within the county's water system. What started as a limited problem quickly escalated into a full-blown crisis. Not only have animals in the local farms been affected, but every resident who turns on a tap puts his or her life at risk. To say that the water is unsafe is an understatement. It is a crime that this happened, and a full-scale investigation is needed now to determine what went wrong. Only then will we fully understand why incompetence took over a relatively simple solution.

1. Think of a current topic, possibly one currently in the news. Write an editorial, presenting your point of view on the topic. Think about what you want to say, and how you will write it, convincing the readers of your stand.

   _____

   _____

   _____

   _____

   _____

   _____

   _____

   _____

2. Now, take the opposing view to the editorial you wrote. Write an editorial with this new stand.

   _____

   _____

   _____

   _____

   _____

   _____

 Select examples of what you consider good and poor editorials. Explain to a friend why you selected what you did.

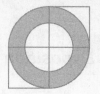

Informative Writing

Advertising

Advertisements try to sell something, or give information on a topic or product.

Persuasive language is used in ads. Look at this example.

> **Advertisements** often *play* with language, by not using full sentences, for instance. This is acceptable, especially if it helps to sell the product or idea.

Tasty. Scrumptious. Extraordinary.
A new mouth-watering sensation.
Destiny.
The candy with zest.
One bite and your mouth will explode
in a blast of sweetness.
Try *Destiny*.
It's waiting on your horizon.

1. Write a different **advertisement** for *Destiny*. Make the parents of children who might want the candy your audience.

_____

_____

_____

_____

_____

_____

_____

_____

_____

_____

2. Write an **advertisement** telling about an upcoming concert or some other such event. Be sure to include all important information.

_____

_____

_____

_____

_____

_____

_____

_____

_____

_____

 Collect examples of effective advertisements. What do you feel makes them effective?

Informative Writing

Exposition

Exposition is writing that gives an explanation of something. Think of an article that tells about a favourite actor in a movie magazine, or a description of how a volcano erupts. These are examples of expository writing.

> An **exposition** is often an essay. It communicates information about an event or topic. Expository writing is formal in style. It presents information, without presenting an opinion.

1. Write an **expository paragraph** on one of the following topics.
   **a favourite television program   riding a skateboard   ordering in a restaurant
   making a lunch   a new discovery   what should be in a locker**

   _____

   _____

   _____

   _____

   _____

   _____

   _____

   _____

   _____

2. Write a short **exposition** on a topic of your choice. Make it at least two paragraphs in length.

   _____

   _____

   _____

   _____

   _____

   _____

   _____

   _____

   _____

   _____

   _____

   _____

   _____

   _____

   _____

   _____

   _____

   _____

   _____

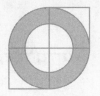

Creative Writing

Description

Description puts images into words. Good description creates vivid images in the reader's mind. Examine this description of a morning street scene.

> **Descriptive writing** should be imaginative and make the reader see what is being described. Use adjectives and other descriptive words. Be observant!

Sunlight crept along the roadway, lighting the shadows, sending them scurrying into the dark corners of the buildings. Birds moved and sang as the day started. A breeze wafted down the street, blowing leaves and garbage in the soft light, as the day opened and took hold.

Descriptive words, metaphors, and other techniques such as personification are used to create a realistic scene.

1. Use **descriptive words** and **phrases** as you describe a pet you have or would like to have.

    _____

    _____

    _____

    _____

    _____

2. Write a **description** (of at least two paragraphs) about a time when you walked into a new room in a building. Create a mind picture for your reader. Picture yourself walking through the room again, noticing the details in the room. Make these part of your description.

    _____

    _____

    _____

    _____

    _____

    _____

    _____

    _____

    _____

    _____

    _____

    _____

    _____

    _____

    _____

    _____

    _____

    _____

 Write a description of what your bedroom usually looks like. Be imaginative!

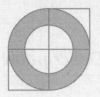

Creative Writing

Narrative

A **narrative** is a story. A short story and a novel are examples of narratives. Some narratives are personal stories about actual incidents or memories in our past. These are true stories, with some fiction mixed in (such as what people *actually* said).

Write a short **narrative** on this page about a memory you have from a past time in your life. Think about what was happening at the time, where you were, what age you were, who was part of the memory, and so on. You could start the narrative with a beginning that sets the reader directly in the time, with an opening such as, "I remember a time when we were..." and so on. See the memory in your mind, and then write what you see.

_____

_____

_____

_____

_____

_____

_____

_____

_____

_____

_____

_____

_____

_____

_____

_____

_____

_____

_____

_____

_____

▶▶ *Write a narrative about an incident that occurred in the present.*

Creative Writing

Short Story: Form

A **short story** is fictional narrative prose. It has many of the characteristics of a novel, but in a much shorter format. Short stories have certain characteristics:

- **plot line:** the sequence of events that follows a **beginning**, **middle**, and **end**, with the action rising to a point of **climax** in the plot, followed by a **resolution** where the author ties up loose ends and finishes the story;

- **conflict:** created by having **character** vs. character, character vs. society, character vs. nature, or inner conflict (such as telling the truth about something or lying); this is what often drives the story, and thus the **plot**;

- **setting:** used to create **conflict**, develop **character**, develop **atmosphere** and **mood**, or to help develop the story's **theme** (the theme is not stated directly; you infer it from the story itself, such as people surviving an earthquak*e* in a nature disaster story);

- **characterization:** often the characterizations are created by the author having the **characters** react to the incidents in the story; characters include the **protagonist** (main character of the story) and **antagonist** (character who struggles against the main character).

When planning a short story, it is a good idea to think about some of these ideas:

- **theme:** the **idea** you wish to present in your story, such as a conflict between two characters being played out within a given setting, and so on;

- **genre:** the **type of story** you will write—adventure? humorous? science fiction? real-life? and so on;

- **plot: what** happens in the story; **where** it begins, **how** it progresses through the middle, and **how** it will end;

- **characters:** who you wish to have in your story—one character? two? main characters and minor characters; what your characters will be like—villains? heroes? funny? depressed? and so on; what the characters will look and be like—older? young? rich? poor? and so on.

- **setting:** where your story takes **place** and what **time** (as in era—older times? historical? present day? and so on).

Use the rest of this page and part of the next page to plan out a short story on a topic of your choice. Use the ideas presented above to help you.

Setting: _____

_____

Plot (plan out the events in your story, including conflicts): _____

_____

_____

_____

_____

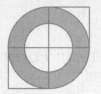

Creative Writing

Plot (continued): _____

_____

_____

_____

Characters: _____

_____

_____

_____

Theme: _____

_____

_____

Now you are ready to write a **first draft** of your short story. Use the rest of this page and the next page to write your story.

_____

_____

_____

_____

_____

_____

_____

_____

_____

_____

_____

_____

_____

_____

_____

Creative Writing

_____

_____

_____

_____

_____

_____

_____

_____

_____

_____

_____

_____

_____

_____

_____

_____

_____

_____

_____

_____

_____

_____

_____

_____

_____

_____

_____

_____

_____

_____

_____

_____

Use the editing phase of the writing process on your story. Have a friend proofread your draft, correct any errors, then produce your final copy in typed form.

Creative Writing

Poetry is a very personal type of writing. It can be structured in style, such as following a definite **rhythm** and **rhyme**, or very casual, such as a **free-verse** poem. Poems look different than any other type of writing. They are written in **stanzas** or **verses** instead of full sentences and paragraphs. One aspect of poetry is the heavy use of **imagery**, where the poet creates an image of something, using creative language that often appeals to the reader's senses. Look at this **haiku** for its use of imagery.

> **Snow drifting on leaves**
> **Falling softly from the clouds**
> **Gathers at my feet**

When you write a poem, think of creative ways to say what you want to say. Use imagery and interesting word choice to create an effect for your reader.

Write a poem, using whatever style you wish. The poem could be a description of something, such as a tree or an event, or about your feelings. Practise your poem ideas in the first section of lines, then rewrite the poem in better form underneath.

> **Poetry writing** can involve creative approaches to grammar: capital letters can be ignored; punctuation can be played with; some words can have inventive spelling, if this fits the poem. Be creative in your writing; experiment with your words and approach to writing your poems.

_____

_____

_____

_____

_____

_____

_____

_____

_____

_____

_____

_____

_____

_____

_____

_____

_____

_____

_____

▶ *Make a collection of your poems in a personal poetry anthology. Share your favourite ones with some friends.*

CHECK UP 1 ▸ *The Writing Process*

1. What are the major steps in the **writing process**? Describe what is done during each step.

    _____

    _____

    _____

    _____

    _____

    _____

    _____

    _____

2. What does it mean to **write for an audience**?

    _____

    _____

    _____

3. When do you know that it is time to produce your **final copy**? _____

    _____

    _____

4. How many **steps** of the writing process must be done for every piece of writing? Explain your answer.

    _____

    _____

    _____

    _____

5. Give reasons for keeping an **ideas journal** for writing.

    _____

    _____

    _____

    _____

    _____

6. Make a list of ways of getting **information** for a piece of writing. Explain the benefit of each.

    _____

    _____

    _____

    _____

    _____

    _____

    _____

CHECK UP 2 ▸ *Paragraphs*

1. Explain these terms in reference to **paragraph writing**.

   unity: _____

   _____

   coherence: _____

   _____

   emphasis: _____

   _____

2. Write a **descriptive paragraph** on one of these topics.

   a sunrise   a sunset   the beach   a new house   concert crowd   exam jitters

   _____

   _____

   _____

   _____

   _____

   _____

   _____

   _____

3. Write a **paragraph** on a topic of your choice. Keep in mind the three terms from Activity #1.

   _____

   _____

   _____

   _____

   _____

   _____

   _____

   _____

   _____

1. Describe these five types of **informative writing**, giving some characteristics of each.

   Essay: _____
   _____
   _____

   Business Letter: _____
   _____
   _____

   Personal Letter: _____
   _____
   _____

   Exposition: _____
   _____
   _____

   Advertisement: _____
   _____
   _____

2. Describe the characteristics of an **editorial**. _____
   _____
   _____

3. Write a short **editorial** on a topic of your choice. Identify the **audience** the editorial is directed at and the **topic** before you write it.

   Audience for Editorial: _____

   Editorial Topic: _____

   Editorial: _____
   _____
   _____
   _____
   _____
   _____
   _____
   _____
   _____
   _____
   _____
   _____
   _____
   _____
   _____

1. What are the characteristics of these two types of writing:

   Descriptive: _____

   _____

   Narrative: _____

   _____

2. Write a short **narrative paragraph** on a topic of your choice.

   _____

   _____

   _____

   _____

   _____

   _____

   _____

   _____

3. Describe each of these **short story** components.

   Setting: _____

   _____

   Plot: _____

   _____

   Characterization: _____

   _____

3. What are some **conflicts** that might appear in a short story?

   _____

   _____

   _____

4. Explain what the **resolution** is in a short story. _____

   _____

5. Write a short **poem** on a topic of your choice.

   _____

   _____

   _____

   _____

   _____

   _____

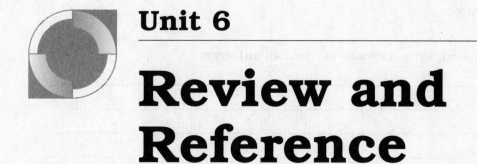

Unit 6

Review and Reference

Review

1. A **prefix** goes on the _____ of a base form, while a **suffix** goes on the _____ of a base form.

2. For these words, underline the **prefixes** and circle the **suffixes**.

   hypersensitivity   restless   childhood   reaction   inferiority   unclassify misinterpret

3. For each word, write a **synonym**, then an **antonym**.

   farther: _____, _____

   backward: _____, _____

   within: _____, _____

   achieve: _____, _____

   successful: _____, _____

4. Use each **homonym pair** in a sentence that shows their usage correctly.

   E.g.: (there, their) Their books are over there, on the table.

   (cymbal, symbol): _____

   _____

   (flour, flower): _____

   _____

   (sense, cents): _____

   _____

   (guessed, guest): _____

   _____

   (presence, presents): _____

   _____

5. Match the following words with the **idioms** below.

   inevitable   challenge   satisfy   disturb

   rock the boat: _____   tall order: _____

   hit the spot: _____   in the cards: _____

   Use two of the **idioms** in sentences that show their meanings.

   (a) _____

   _____

   (b) _____

   _____

Review

1. **Clichés** are tired, worn-out phrases, such as **to the bitter end** (means: the end). They should be used only on occasion. Match the clichés with their actual meanings.

    a shock   do it   early morning   cold   stable   stopped

    (a) nipped in the bud:_____   (d) a bolt from the blue: _____

    (b) at the crack of dawn: _____   (e) solid as a rock:_____

    (c) as cold as ice: _____   (f) bit the bullet:_____

    Now use one of the clichés in a sentence to show its meaning.

    _____

    _____

2. **Proverbs** are wise sayings that writers sometimes use to illustrate a point, such as: **You can lead a horse to water, but you can't make him drink** (means: You can't always make someone do something.). Write what you think these proverbs mean.

    (a) Early to bed, early to rise, makes one healthy, wealthy, and wise. _____

    _____

    (b) The early bird gets the worm. _____

    _____

    (c) Great minds think alike. _____

3. **Jargon** is language that is particular to a certain sector of society, such as computer jargon: **modem, software, RAM, nanosecond**. Write a sentence that uses jargon that you know from a certain sector of society that you are familiar with (such as music or sports jargon).

    _____

    _____

4. Write a short paragraph on a topic of your choice in **formal language**. Rewrite it in **informal language**.

    _____

    _____

    _____

    _____

    _____

    _____

    _____

    _____

Review

1. Think about what you do to **spell words correctly**. Write down your methods in a couple of sentences.

   _____

   _____

   _____

   _____

2. Divide these words into **syllables**. Place the accent over the stressed syllable.

   vocabulary:_____   resources:_____

   geography: _____   stationary: _____

   bibliography: _____   international: _____

3. Circle the **misspelled words** in these sentences. Rewrite each sentence with the correctly spelled words.

   (a) Into the vallei thay went, gatheriing speede as they rushed dowm the hill like a herd of antulope.

   _____

   _____

   (b) "Sevuntene people saw my act, and not one of thwm aplauded," sighd the actor.

   _____

   _____

   (c) A way to get attention is by doing somthing consisdered outrageours and diferent from what you normally do!

   _____

   _____

4. Write two sentences on topics of your choice. Read back through the sentence **checking for spelling**. Circle any words you think are misspelled. Check them in a dictionary. Rewrite your sentences if necessary.

   _____

   _____

   _____

   _____

   _____

   _____

Review

1. **Capital letters** are to be used on proper nouns, such as Winnipeg, Maria, Pacific, Jupiter, Toyota. Make a list of ten proper nouns. Use capital letters correctly.

   _____

   _____

   _____

2. Read these sentences. Circle any letters that should be capitalized. Rewrite the sentences with proper use of **capital letters**.

   (a) we journey down the amazon river on a boat called *discoverer*.

   _____

   (b) The brazilian guides were very helpful as we tried to find dr. mallory's camp.

   _____

   (c) i knew that we had to get to him before wednesday april 24 as he would run out of supplies by then.

   _____

   (d) a few days out, we were told that the doctor had gone westward toward the andes.

   _____

   (e) Jerome, kali, and raoul suggested that we head back to rio de janeiro before friday.

   _____

3. Make lists using the following as themes. Use **capital letters** where necessary.

   (a) Favourite Singers or Groups: _____

   _____

   (b) Favourite Television Programs: _____

   _____

   (c) Favourite Movies: _____

   _____

   (d) Favourite Games: _____

   _____

4. Select one of your lists from Activity #3. Explain why they are your favourites. Use **capital letters** where necessary.

   _____

   _____

   _____

Review

(NOTE: You may want to review how commas, colons, and semicolons are used by reading the examples on pp. 64 and 66.)

1. **Commas** are used to make writing clear to the reader, as well as to give a chance to pause. Place commas in these sentences where you think they are needed.

   (a) Josiah wanted rags buckets a supply of water and towels for the car wash.

   (b) Whenever they came to our parties they always seemed to make the festivities go sour.

   (c) A very tall hot-air balloon drifted over the buildings hovered above the City Hall then sailed away toward the desert.

   (d) I frequently attend rock concerts not because I have lots of money but more for the enjoyment and energy that I feel at these events.

   (e) Why can't we be ready to pack our bags get in the car and drive ten hours all the way back home just so that we can see the next episode of *Drake's House*?

2. **Colons** and **semicolons** are used to separate lists and clauses. Insert colons and semicolons where you feel they are needed in these sentences.

   (a) We want you to get these things hammers, nails, saws, planes, sandpaper, and a very large box of insulation.

   (b) I hoped the worst was over evidently I was wrong.

   (c) Many cheering fans stormed the team's locker room they got out just in time.

   (d) Here's what we do we climb the wall and make like gazelles for the gate.

   (e) Try to pay attention it's the least that you can do.

3. Write a short paragraph on a topic of your choice. Use **commas**, **colons**, and **semicolons** in your paragraph.

   _____

   _____

   _____

   _____

   _____

   _____

   _____

   _____

   _____

   _____

   _____

(NOTE: You may want to review how quotation marks, quotation punctuation, dashes, parentheses, brackets, and diagonals are used by reading the examples on pp. 67, 68, and 69.)

1. Rewrite these sentences adding **quotation marks** and **punctuation** where necessary.

   (a) We didn't get a chance to try the ferris wheel complained Lorraine

   _____

   (b) That was a great speech said Senator Chai I think you have a chance of winning this election

   _____

   (c) The captain asked Coach why do we have to practise after we have won the game

   _____

   (d) I rarely know the answer the giant sighed I guess I just can't think up this high

   _____

2. Write a sentence that uses **quotation marks** and proper **quotation punctuation**.

   _____

   _____

3. Rewrite these sentences adding **dashes**, **parentheses**, **brackets**, and **diagonals** where needed.

   (a) I hear that we receive a pass fail mark on this test, not a percentage.

   _____

   (b) If only I had listened to them at the station and filled up with gas

   _____

   (c) Before you leave, make sure you have 1 a fresh sheet of paper, 2 a working pen, and 3 a clear mind ready to write the best answers of your life.

   _____

   _____

   (d) At one point I yelled out, "Don't forget that it was all of them student council members that voted for this!"

   _____

   _____

   (e) The game the only one they would win was not covered by the media.

   _____

   _____

Review

1. **Nouns** can be **common** (girl) or **proper** (Sharlene). For each noun listed, write a common or proper noun that could be paired with it.

   river: _____   Atlantic: _____

   friend: _____   mountain: _____

   team: _____   Jason: _____

2. Complete these sentences by writing a **pronoun** for each **boldfaced** noun.

   (a) The **train** entered the tunnel, but _____ didn't exit.

   (b) Many **lions** at the zoo were roaming the field, and _____ didn't look happy.

   (c) When **Tony** played for the **crowd**, _____ knew _____ always sang along.

3. Write a sentence that shows proper **noun-pronoun agreement**.

   _____

   _____

4. Verbs can be **active voice** (He played the game) or **passive voice** (The game was played by him). Indicate **active** or **passive** for the verbs in each of these sentences.

   (a) The plane landed safely on the runway. _____

   (b) Passengers were led to the rooms by the attendants._____

   (c) Everyone sighed with relief that the ordeal was over. _____

5. Now, rewrite each sentence in its opposite voice (For example, a sentence with the **active voice** would be rewritten in the **passive voice**.)

   (a) _____

   (b) _____

   (c) _____

6. Verb tense is often **past** (He played the game), **present** (He plays the game), or **future** (He will play the game). Rewrite each of these sentences in the verb tense indicated.

   (a) They run the course every day.

   Future:_____

   (b) The horse leaps over his stall.

   Past: _____

   (c) A cool breeze blew over the meadow.

   Present:_____

Review

Parts of Speech 2

1. Verbs can be **transitive** (He threw the football.) or **intransitive** (She runs quickly.) or **copula** (This soap smells fresh.) Identify the type of verb in each of the following sentences.

   (a) He enjoyed the seafood at the new restaurant. _____

   (b) Our dog eats ice cubes on hot days. _____

   (c) The girls' relay team won the medal. _____

   (d) This dessert tastes delicious. _____

   (e) Have you seen the giant moose? _____

   (f) The Canada Geese flew noisily overhead. _____

   (g) He reads very quickly. _____

   (h) She is a teacher who understands students very well. _____

   (i) Her car is a standard. _____

   (j) The bank manager walked into the vault. _____

   (k) The city grew quickly. _____

2. Rewrite each of the sentences, changing the verb to another verb form, such as from **intransitive** to **transitive** or **copula**.

   (a) _____

   (b) _____

   (c) _____

   (d) _____

   (e) _____

   (f) _____

   (g) _____

   (h) _____

   (i) _____

   (j) _____

   (k) _____

Review

1. A **verbal** is a verb used as a part of speech other than a verb. Verbals can be **infinitives** (**To win** is the team's wish), **participles** (Ours is a **winning** team), or **gerunds** (**Winning** is all they ever do). Indicate the type for each **boldfaced** verbal in the following sentences.

    (a) **To jump** is every trampoline artist's goal._____

    (b) Jasmine has a **smiling** face every time we see her. _____

    (c) **Running** is what cheetahs do very well. _____

2. Now, write one sentence for each type of **verbal**.

    (a) **Infinitive:** _____

    _____

    (b) **Participle:** _____

    _____

    (c) **Gerund:** _____

    _____

3. **Adjectives** are words that describe nouns or pronouns (the **colourful** wall). Adjectives can be words or phrases. Write adjectives that could be used to describe each of these words. Remember that colours and numbers can be adjectives.

    sailboat: _____

    dirt bike: _____

    vacation: _____

4. **Adverbs** are words that describe verbs, adjectives, or other adverbs. They often end in **-ly** and answer the questions How, When, Where (ran **slowly**; played **at ten o'clock**). Adverbs can be words or phrases. Write adverbs that could be used to describe each of these words.

    walked: _____

    parked: _____

    stayed: _____

5. Write two sentences on topics of your choice. Use **adjectives** and **adverbs** in each sentence. They may be words or phrases or a mixture of both.

    (a) _____

    _____

    (b) _____

    _____

Review

1. Identify each of these sentences as **declarative**, **interrogative**, **imperative**, or **exclamatory**.

   (a) We won the game in overtime! _____

   (b) The cheers rang through the rafters that night. _____

   (c) Where was the defence when it was needed? _____

   (d) Get your hot dogs while they're hot! _____

2. Write an example of each: **declarative**, **interrogative**, **imperative**, and **exclamatory** sentences.

   (a) _____

   (b) _____

   (c) _____

   (d) _____

3. Each **sentence** is made up of a **subject** (Who or What the sentence is about) and a **predicate** (the verb; what the subject does). Draw a line between the subject and predicate in each sentence.

   (a) The towering column of smoke billowed from the office tower during the afternoon rush hour.

   (b) We tried to stop the charging buffalo.

4. A **simple sentence** has a **subject** and a **predicate** (The class wrote the exam). Add a subject or predicate to each of these sentence parts to make simple sentences.

   (a) The passenger plane _____

   (b) _____ walked into the store with some cash.

   (c) _____ had played the game well.

   (d) A very impatient customer _____

5. A **compound sentence** is made from two simple sentences (The boy went to the store and he bought some candy). Compound sentences join the simple sentences with **conjunctions**. Rewrite this pair of simple sentences as a compound sentence. Remember to use a conjunction to join the sentences.

   The crowd watched the parade. It went right by them.

   _____

   _____

6. Now, write your own **compound sentence**. Make sure it is made from two simple sentences.

   _____

   _____

Review

Sentences 2

1. A **clause** is a group of words that has a **subject** and a **predicate**. A **main clause** can stand on its own as a sentence (I want to go to the show). A **subordinate clause** cannot stand on its own as a sentence (Whenever I want to go to the show). Identify whether each of these is a main clause or a subordinate clause.

   (a) The whistle blew to end the shift. _____

   (b) When the crowd cheered for him _____

   (c) As we approached the side of the castle _____

   (d) A growling sound rolled across the room. _____

   (e) When the cat jumped over his head _____

2. A **complex sentence** has one main clause and one or more subordinate clauses (When the bell rang, she ran into the house). Add the appropriate clauses to these to make complex sentences.

   (a) _____, he won the lottery.

   (b) The movie house was filled with laughter _____

   (c) _____, the day ended.

   (d) _____, we tried again.

   (e) A fearful antelope eyed the lion, _____

3. A **compound-complex sentence** has two or more main clauses and one or more subordinate clauses (I had fun today, and my day really began when I went to the summer carnival.). Add the appropriate clauses to these to make compound-complex sentences.

   (a) The storm moved over the land, _____

   (b) A heavy load fell off the cart, _____

   (c) _____, after we had finished painting the house.

4. Write a **complex sentence** on a topic of your choice.

   _____

5. Write a **compound-complex sentence** on a topic of your choice.

   _____

Review

1. Read the following. Rewrite any that are **sentence fragments**, completing them to make sentences.

   (a) Suddenly, the ship hit a sandbar, sending passengers and crew sprawling across the deck.

   (b) The captain and his officers.

   (c) The first officer with the rest of the bridge crew.

   _____

   _____

   _____

2. Fix these **comma splices** and **run-on sentences**. Rewrite them as correct sentences.

   (a) The players assembled on the field, it was their first game of the season.

   _____

   (b) At the whistle, the ball went into play the opposing team scored the first points.

   _____

3. Check these sentences for **subject-verb agreement**. Rewrite any that don't seem correct.

   (a) Jerrold will plays with the rest of the club as they gets ready for the games.

   _____

   (b) How many wants hot dogs and who want a hamburger?

   _____

4. Check these sentences for **modifier** problems. Rewrite them, making sure the modifiers are describing the correct things.

   (a) Many trains leave stations every day that need mechanical repairs.

   _____

   (b) This restaurant serves meals to patrons that are inexpensive.

   _____

5. Rewrite this sentence which has a **double negative** and a **split infinitive** so that its meaning is clear.

   No people are not allowed to diagonally walk across this street.

   _____

   _____

Review

A **paragraph** is a set of sentences that expresses and supports a topic or idea. It usually has a topic sentence that sets out what the main idea is. Other sentences support the topic sentence. A paragraph ends with a good concluding sentence. Read this example.

The day had come for the test. Everyone in the room had studied for days. Many had tried to stay awake for hours on end, trying to cram more information into their minds. Nothing mattered now, though. They were here to write the test, and only a few would pass.

1. Write a paragraph on one of the following topics. Make your paragraph at least four to five sentences long.

   watching a comedian   a commercial   the painting   making a sandwich   the gift

   _____

   _____

   _____

   _____

   _____

   _____

2. Write two or three paragraphs on a topic of your choice. Make sure that your paragraphs link together correctly, supporting the main ideas presented.

   _____

   _____

   _____

   _____

   _____

   _____

   _____

   _____

   _____

   _____

   _____

   _____

   _____

One type of **informative writing** is the essay. An **essay** has three main parts: **introduction**, **body**, and **conclusion**. An essay is usually an opinion writing where the author presents a point of view based on a thesis statement (main idea of the essay) and the ideas that come from it. Practise writing ideas for an essay on this page.

1. **Introduction of the Essay:** Think of an essay topic. It could be an opinion on something such as: how to get a job; fairness in sports; tests in secondary school; school rules; and so on. Brainstorm some ideas on a sheet of paper, then write your essay topic here.
   Topic: _____

   Now, write a thesis statement to give your essay its main idea. The thesis statement should give some indication of what your point of view will be on the subject.

   Thesis Statement: _____

   _____

2. **Body of the Essay:** Write some ideas that you could pursue in your essay. They can be written in point form or in full sentences. They should present ideas that outline your argument, and lead the reader to what your point of view is.

   _____

   _____

   _____

   _____

   _____

   _____

   _____

   _____

3. **Conclusion of the Essay:** Write some ideas that could be included in your conclusion. These should draw your essay ideas together in such a way that your opinion on the topic is very clear to the reader.

   _____

   _____

   _____

   _____

   _____

   _____

Now you have your essay planned. You could use these ideas to write the essay in full.

Review

Informative writing is often used to persuade readers to a particular viewpoint (such as in an essay). Three such types of writings are advertisements, speeches, and editorials. On this page, write the outline for a speech, copy for an ad, or an editorial on a topic of your choice, or one from below. For an explanation of these types of writing, read the examples given on pp. 121, 123, and 124.

Sample Topics: **a new toothpaste   problems in government   violence at games**

a new type of music   learning to drive   completing a project   vacations

_____

_____

_____

_____

_____

_____

_____

_____

_____

_____

_____

_____

_____

_____

_____

_____

_____

_____

_____

_____

_____

_____

_____

_____

_____

_____

Review

On this page, write a **descriptive** or a **narrative** piece of writing. (For an explanation of these types of writing, read over the examples on pp. 126 and 127.) Think about what you want to describe or tell about. Remember that a narrative is a story, and a description describes a thing, place, and so on. Be creative! Use your imagination. You may want to add an illustration to your writing as well.

_____

_____

_____

_____

_____

_____

_____

_____

_____

_____

_____

_____

_____

_____

_____

_____

_____

_____

_____

_____

_____

_____

_____

_____

Review

On this page, write a **short story** or a **poem** on a topic of your choice. Remember to be as creative as you can in your approach to this type of writing. Use imaginative ideas. Try different poetic styles, such as free verse or rhythm-rhyme. You may wish to illustrate your writing.

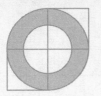

Editing and Proofreading Guide

All writing needs to be **edited** and **proofread**. **Editing** includes proofreading your work (checking it for errors) and making sure the words and ideas flow properly. After you finish a piece of writing, read it over to check that it makes sense. Give it to a friend to read. Ask for honest feedback. You may have to rewrite sections to make your ideas clearer to the reader.

When you **proofread**, check for errors in spelling, capitalization, punctuation, grammar, usage, and the look of the writing. The following checklist will help as you edit your work, or that of a friend.

Editing Checklist

Punctuation
✓ Have I used periods
  • at the end of each statement?
  • after abbreviations?
  • after a person's initials?
✓ Have I used question marks after questions?
✓ Have I used exclamation marks after words or sentences that show strong emotion (but not too often)?
✓ Have I used commas
  • between names and parts of addresses?
  • between parts of dates?
  • between items in a series?
  • after introductory adverbial clauses that begin a sentence but are not a vital part of it?
  • after words used in direct address ("Ravi, it is time to go.")?
  • after a subordinate clause when it begins a sentence?
  • between parts of a compound sentence?
✓ Have I used apostrophes
  • in contractions to show missing letters?
  • to show possession?
✓ Have I used quotation marks
  • to enclose a direct quotation?
  • to enclose the title of short works, such as poems, stories, and songs?
✓ Have I underlined (when handwriting) or italicized (when using a computer) book, film, and television series titles, and names of newspapers and magazines?

Capitalization
✓ Have I capitalized
  • the first word in each sentence?
  • names of people, titles when used with a name, buildings, organizations, cities, provinces, countries?
  • names of political parties, historical events, religions?
  • names of months, days of the week, holidays?
  • the pronoun "I"?

Spelling
✓ Have I used a dictionary/spell checker to confirm the spelling of those words about which I'm unsure?

Grammar
✓ Is there agreement between the subject and the verb in my sentences?
✓ Are my verb tenses consistent and correct?
✓ Have I used the correct past tense of irregular verbs?
✓ Is the person to whom each pronoun refers clear?
✓ Does each pronoun agree with its antecedent?
✓ Are subject and object forms of pronouns (who, whom) used correctly?

Usage
✓ Have frequently confused words been used correctly (red, read)?

Preparing the Manuscript
✓ Is my draft neat, double-spaced with 2.5-cm (one-inch) margins around the text?
✓ Did I indent the first line of each paragraph or double-space between my paragraphs?
✓ Do I have the page number in the upper right-hand corner of every page after the first?
✓ Does my cover sheet show the title, my name and class number, the date, and my teacher's name?
✓ Did I proofread my paper one last time for errors?

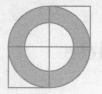

Using Reference Materials

Reference materials are used to give us information on a variety of subjects.

Dictionary

A dictionary gives the spelling of a word, its meanings, part of speech, usage, and often its history (etymology). Dictionary entries appear in **alphabetical order**. Each dictionary page has guide words at the top. The first guide word tells us the first word that appears on the page; the second tells us the last word that appears on the page. For example, circle the words that would appear on a dictionary page with the guide words **depot—desert:**

despot   deputy   desertion   depose   deplete   dessert   derive   desperate   decision   depth

Thesaurus

A thesaurus entry will list synonyms of a given word, with any antonyms or related (similar) words. Words in a thesaurus are usually in **alphabetical order**. To look up a word, use the guide words at the top of the pages, or the **index** at the back of the book. Look at this sample thesaurus entry.

HUMBLE	*adjective*	common, courteous, docile, homespun, insignificant, low, lowly, modest, obedient, polite, respectful
	antonyms	assertive, important, proud
	verb	abash, break, bring down, chasten, conquer, humiliate
	antonym	raise

Use the thesaurus to choose the word that is right for your purpose and make your writing more interesting. For example, not all of the words in the above example would be suitable for every type of writing: **"He is a *humble* man,"** has a slightly different meaning than **"He is a *polite* man."**

Reference Sources

You can use many of the following when looking for information:

- **Reference Books and CD-ROMs:** Encyclopedias, almanacs, fact books, quotation books, yearbooks, and atlases can all be found in your library's Reference section.

- **The Internet:** This global network lets you access information Web sites through your computer. It is an excellent way to get data fast, 24 hours a day.

- **Vertical files:** These are collections of pictures, news clippings, brochures, and pamphlets that have been put in files and stored in filing cabinets. They are usually organized alphabetically by subject.

- **Microfilm:** This is a storage system that uses film containing the reduced images of newspapers and magazines. Special projector-like machines are used to view the microfilm.

- **Non-Print Resources:** This includes audio and videotapes, photographs, films and filmstrips, CDs, records, and so on.

- **Community Agencies:** This includes pamphlets and other material from the community, and government documents, information, and other materials. Many of these materials are available at the information and reference desks of libraries.

Information can also be gathered from people by **interviews** and **questionnaires**. This often gives the researcher first-hand knowledge of an event and can add realism to a piece of writing. Include yourself in this! Diary or journal entries are often used in writing, giving a personal touch to the piece.

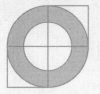

Using the Internet for Research

The Internet is a global network of Web sites. It is accessed through your computer. To get connected to the Internet, you need a **modem** (cable or telephone line) and an **Internet service provider.** Once connected, you will be able to get onto the **World Wide Web**. This is a network of computers that stores **Web pages**, or Web sites. Each Web site has a Web address, usually given in this manner: **www.pearsoned.com** The three **w**'s indicate that the site is on the World Wide Web. The second part indicates the homepage (in this example Pearson Education). The **.com** indicates a company, and is the end of the address. The pages are connected to each other through **hyperlinks**. These links take you to new Web pages that usually have something in common with the site you were at. Each site could have everything from text to pictures to audio and video files. To browse the site, you click on a highlighted line, picture, or icon. You are instantly taken to that section of the site. Items at the site can be printed out or saved on your computer's hard drive.

Surfing the Web can be enjoyable, but it's better if you have an idea of what you are looking for. Use key words that can be searched for by a **search engine**. A search engine is an organizing feature of the Internet. Yahoo!, AltaVista, Google, and Lycos are examples of search engines. Load one by typing in its address (such as **www.yahoo.com**) then go to the Search box. Type in the item you are searching for, then click on **Search**. The search engine will "search" the World Wide Web for sites that match your item. It will eventually turn up **hits—sites** that have something to do with your request. Often, too many sites turn up and it's difficult to know what to look at. It's a good idea to be specific in your search. For example, if you want information on **dogs**, determine: is it a particular dog? Typing in **German Shepherd dogs** will give you more specific sites related to your search than just **dogs**.

Here is an example of a Web page from the publishing company that produced this book.

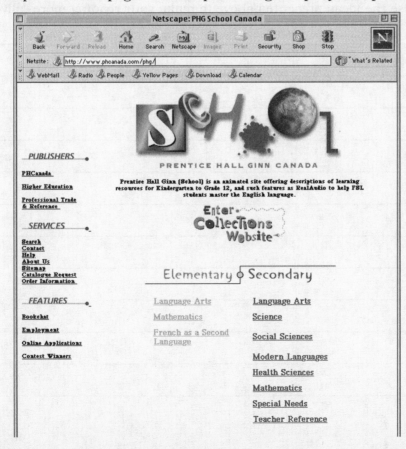

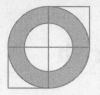

Reading Your Work Out Loud

Often, we write something, only to find that the ideas didn't quite come out right. One way to check your work is to **read it out loud**. This could include reading it to a friend or to yourself. When we hear the piece read, we often pick up things that may have seemed good in the writing but don't work in the retelling. Another reason to read your work out loud is to share it with a larger audience. Here are some things to think about when you read your work aloud.

- **Volume of voice**: Make sure your voice can be heard by all, but is not so loud that it is irritating.

- **Intonation**: This is the way you use tone of voice when you read your work. Does your voice go up a little when you read a question? Do you add feeling when you come to a part that is happy or sad? Remember to use your tone of voice correctly as you read.

- **Pace**: This is the speed at which you read your work. Don't go too fast, but don't go too slow either. Find the correct pace for the piece you are reading.

As you read, make eye contact at times with your audience. This will mean raising your eyes from the paper, but it will add to the reading. Move your gaze to different parts of the audience. You will make them feel you are looking directly at them, and including them in your reading in a more personal way. After reading, listen to comments from the audience, especially if the reading was to try out a piece you needed checked. Be open to their ideas: they might improve your writing in ways you hadn't thought of.

Write a short piece on a topic of your choice. Read it out loud to yourself, then to a friend or group of friends. Use the ideas presented above to make your reading more "alive."

_____

_____

_____

_____

_____

_____

_____

_____

_____

_____

_____

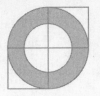

Self-Evaluation Sheet

It is always a good idea to **evaluate** your work. This will help you look critically at what you have written or done as a project or other assignment. Use the following form to guide you as you self-evaluate.

Rating Your Work

Use a rating scale to answer the following items.

Rating Scale: 3 = very much

2 = somewhat

1 = no or not at all

1. Did you plan out your work? _____

2. Did you use a variety of resource materials, if applicable? _____

3. Did you share your work with a friend or others in its early stage? _____

4. Did you incorporate changes based on constructive comments from others? _____

5. Did your work turn out as you expected? _____

6. Did you enjoy doing this work? _____

7. Are you pleased with the results of your work? _____

Comments

Based on your rating of your work, make comments on what you liked, disliked, and would change if you did this type of work again.

_____

_____

_____

_____

_____

Next Steps

Based on your rating and comments, what would be the next steps you would look at to improve your approach to this type of work in the future?

_____

_____

_____

_____

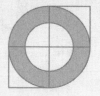

Peer-Evaluation Sheet

We often have peers evaluate our work. This gives us comments from people who are familiar with similar settings that we share, and this can help us as we look objectively at our work. Use the format on this page when you have peers evaluate your work.

Content of the Work

Comments (i.e., what the work is about, interest level, ideas well thought through, and so on):

_____

_____

_____

Structure of the Work

Comments (i.e., follows a logical order of events or ideas, proper grammar and mechanics used throughout, easy to read and follow, and so on):

_____

_____

_____

Good Points about the Work

Comments (i.e., what worked well, what was interesting, what caught your attention, and so on):

_____

_____

_____

Areas to Revise in the Work

Comments (i.e., what needs attention in content, structure, mechanics, spelling, and so on):

_____

_____

_____

Suggestions for Next Steps in the Work

Comments (i.e., best audience the work would appeal to, presentation and look of the work, and so on):

_____

_____

_____

Evaluating Media Works

Use this page when you wish to evaluate a media work, such as a TV program, movie, concert, Web page, or other similar media production.

ITEM REVIEWED: _____

TIME OF REVIEW: _____ **PLACE:** _____

SUMMARY OF ITEM REVIEWED (e.g., TV show, comedy; CD by _____; movie: summarize the main details of the item):

COMMENTS—POSITIVE: _____

_____

_____

_____

_____

COMMENTS—NEGATIVE: _____

_____

_____

_____

_____

COMMENTS—OTHER: _____

_____

_____

_____

_____

SUGGESTIONS FOR IMPROVEMENTS: _____

_____

_____

_____

OVERALL RATING (1: poor; to 5: excellent): _____

161

Interview Sheet

Use this page to organize an interview.

TOPIC: _____   INTERVIEWER: _____

INTERVIEWEE: _____   DATE OF INTERVIEW: _____

TIME/PLACE OF INTERVIEW: _____

PRELIMINARY RESEARCH:

_____

_____

_____

_____

_____

POSSIBLE QUESTIONS/AREAS TO DISCUSS:

_____

_____

_____

REVISED QUESTIONS:

_____

_____

_____

_____

_____

RESPONSES (point form; you may wish to tape the
responses to your questions, or write them in a separate
notebook or sheet of paper):

When taking **notes** during an interview:
• do not write down every word spoken, but make sure you capture the **main points**;
• check the **accuracy** of your notes before quoting your interviewee.

_____

_____

_____

_____

FOLLOW-UP (Further interview necessary; other people to interview on this topic):

_____

_____

_____

Credits

P. 4 Excerpt from *Making History* by Colin M. Bain, Dennis DesRivieres, Peter Flaherty, Donna M. Goodman, Elma Schemenauer, and Angus L. Scully. Copyright © 2000 Pearson Education Canada Inc. Reprinted by permission; **p. 11** Reprinted from *Saturday Night* magazine; **p. 15** (photo) AP/World Wide Photo; **p. 17** Based on "Citizenship in Action: Thelma Chalifoux, Senator" from *Citizenship: Issues and Action* by Mark Evans, Rosemary Evans, Michael Slodovnick, and Terezia Zoric. Copyright © 2000 Pearson Education Canada Inc. Used by permission; **p. 18** Based on "Technology and the Northern Cod" from *Atlantic Canada in the Global Community* by William Butt, James Crewe, Robert Kenyon, Deirdre Kessler, Russell McLean, Dennis Minty, and Elma Schemenauer. Copyright © 1998 Breakwater Books Ltd./Prentice Hall Ginn Canada Inc. Used by permission of Pearson Education Canada Inc. and Breakwater Books Ltd.; **p. 19** Excerpt from *Making History* by Bain, DesRivieres, Flaherty, Goodman, Schemenauer, and Scully. Copyright © 2000 Pearson Education Canada Inc. Reprinted by permission; **p. 21** Excerpt from *Making History* by Bain, DesRivieres, Flaherty, Goodman, Schemenauer, and Scully. Copyright © 2000 Pearson Education Canada Inc. Reprinted by permission; **p. 23** Excerpt from *Making Connections, Canada's Geography* by Bruce W. Clark and John K. Wallace. Copyright © 1999 by Prentice Hall Ginn Canada Inc. Reprinted by permission of Pearson Education Canada Inc.; **p. 25** Excerpt from *Citizenship: Issues and Action* by Evans, Evans, Slodovnick, and Zoric. Copyright © 2000 Pearson Education Canada Inc. Reprinted by permission; **p. 25** (photo) CP Picture Archive/Adrian Wyld; **p. 27** Excerpt from *Making Connections, Canada's Geography* by Clark and Wallace. Copyright © 1999 by Prentice Hall Ginn Canada Inc. Reprinted by permission of Pearson Education Canada Inc.; **p. 29** "Good Eats Guide" by Lori Moore. Reprinted by courtesy of *Teen* magazine (February 1995); **p. 31** Excerpt from *Atlantic Canada in the Global Community* by Butt, Crewe, Kenyon, Kessler, McLean, Minty, and Schemenauer. Copyright © 1998 Breakwater Books Ltd./Prentice Hall Ginn Canada Inc. Used by permission of Pearson Education Canada Inc. and Breakwater Books Ltd.; **p. 33** Copyright © 1995 by Barbara Hager. First published in *The Globe and Mail*.